PRESENTING

Rosa Guy

TUSAS 543

Twayne's United States Authors Series
Young Adult Authors

Ron Brown, General Editor

The Young Adult Authors books seek to
meet the need for critical studies of fiction
for young adults. Each volume examines
the life and work of one author, helping
both teachers and readers of young adult
literature to understand better the writers
they have read with such pleasure
and fascination.

PRESENTING
Rosa Guy

Jerrie Norris

Twayne Publishers • Boston
A Division of G. K. Hall & Co.

Presenting Rosa Guy
Jerrie Norris

Published by Twayne Publishers
A Division of G. K. Hall & Co.
70 Lincoln Street
Boston, Massachusetts 02111

Copyediting supervised by Barbara Sutton.
Book design by Marne Sultz.
Book production by Janet Zietowski.

Typeset in 10/13 Century Schoolbook
by Modern Graphics, Inc., Weymouth, Massachusetts

Printed on permanent/durable acid-free paper
and bound in the United States of America

Library of Congress Cataloging in Publication Data

Norris, Jerrie.
  Presenting Rosa Guy.

  (Twayne's United States authors series ; TUSAS 543. Young adult authors)
  Bibliography: p.
  Includes index.
  Summary: Examines the life and works of the author, born in Trinidad and
raised in Harlem, of such young adult fiction as "Ruby" and "The Friends."
  1. Guy, Rosa—Criticism and interpretation.   2. Young adult fiction,
American—History and criticism. [1. Guy, Rosa—Criticism and
interpretation.   2. American literature—History and criticism]
  I. Title.   II. Series.
PS3557.U93Z76   1988   813'.54 [92]   88-5369
ISBN 0-8057-8207-9

Contents

Preface

My first encounter with Rosa Guy was in the pages of her first young adult novel, *The Friends*. At the time, the name Rosa Guy was simply another author's name to be remembered (or forgotten) in my search for books of interest to my young inner-city readers. By the time I had turned the final page of the novel, however, my curiosity had been stirred.

I wanted to know more about this writer who moved with ease from the street lingo of Harlem to the rhythmic speech of the West Indies. What had prompted her to create the novel's central characters—two young women whose circumstances gave new dimensions to the word *outsider?* How did she create a character like Edith Jackson who seemed a living, breathing part of my own southern-bred, sixties-saturated memories, but who was also fresh and credible to young people? What experiences shaped her vision, which tempered the harshest realities with the hope and resilience of the individual will? Each new book she produced raised more questions, but unfortunately there were few answers to be found in the critical or biographical literature at that time.

Years later I finally met Guy, but I found myself unable to tell her of my long-standing interest in her work. Tall and exotic looking, she seemed perfectly at ease moving among the crush of book-world celebrities and admiring librarians gathered for yet another American Library Association conference party; the same could not be said for me. I was dazzled by the elegant party trappings and the sheer number of authors and artists. Face to face with her, those burning questions seemed to vaporize. Only mundane party conversation and a few mumbled words of praise came to mind. The ball fumbled, four years passed before I had another opportunity to meet Guy.

The second meeting took place without the clink of cocktail glasses or the crush of conference-weary partygoers. In Boston to serve on a young adult writers' panel as part of the 1984 *Boston Globe* Book Festival, she graciously agreed to arrange her schedule to include time for an afternoon interview with me. Arrangements had been made by my friend and editor Ron Brown. I had only to prepare myself for this second chance. Equipped with my tape recorder and four years worth of questions, I made the two-hour flight to Boston, mentally rehearsing how I would handle this opportunity.

Meeting Guy that Sunday in the lobby of Boston's Ritz Carlton Hotel, I was surprised to find that she was not as tall as I remembered. I was also relieved to discover that this meeting would not be a repeat performance of my previously bungled opportunity. Ron Brown and Guy's editor, George Nicholson, are owed much of the credit here. They quickly introduced us and led us off for a well-planned and distraction-free Sunday brunch. The initial exchanges of pleasantries that took place on the short walk to the restaurant relaxed into real conversation over the food. Leaving Ron and George after the meal, Guy and I continued to talk as we walked back to the hotel to begin a two-hour interview session.

During the course of the afternoon the conversation ranged from the West Indian population in Boston to the box-office success of the film *Purple Rain*. Guy's dual heritage, so evident in her writing, was apparent during this conversation and the others that would follow. She spoke of New York with the vocal fervor of a native and criticized the city from a native's viewpoint. She was equally fervent about her Trinidadian heritage. As she remarked on the similarities between the languages of the two locales, her face reflected her feelings; language and heritage were clearly important to her. Within the context of such conversations, her casual but pointedly stated preference for the French pronunciation of her name (*Guy* rhymes with *me*) came as no surprise.

Our discussion was full of revelations, however. More an extended dialogue than an interview, the atmosphere was informal and the course of the conversation fluid. Comfortably sitting on her hotel room bed with a pillow fluffed behind her head, Guy talked freely. She answered questions forthrightly (even when the answer was "I don't tell") and generously shared a wealth of information that was as much social as personal history. Her diverse experiences and the depth of her personal involvement in the events of the sixties, although initially surprising, seemed only natural as she spoke about her life, her aspirations, and her worldview. Her taped response to follow-up questions submitted some months later supplemented the information from the two-hour Boston interview. The tapes, about 2½ hours in length, are the source of all undocumented statements by Guy in the text.

When I reviewed the tapes and my notes, I realized that no tight web of facts about her life emerges from the wealth of information. Specific dates and events were not priorities with her; titles and names sometimes eluded her; and facts like birth and publication dates, when given at all, were often guesstimates. Instead, what I have derived from her comments, her books, and published biographical information is a view of how the writer developed over thirty years of artistic and social change as both participant and observer. This context is crucial, for she has both shaped and been shaped by the times.

The cumulative magic of Guy's books have confirmed my impression when I first encountered her work: Rosa Guy is a true storyteller. Twice-blessed by the African oral tradition through her Trinidadian roots and Harlem upbringing, she writes novels that both entertain and convey the history and culture of a people. Writing out of experiences that are a part of our contemporary lives, she proves E. M. Forster's observation that "fiction is truer than history, because it goes beyond the evidence."[1] The uniquely revealing explorations of society that are integral parts of her novels allow readers to penetrate beyond the evidence of their lives to the universal truths that bind us.

Like her novels, then, Guy's life and work are much more than the sum of the basic facts. I extend my sincere thanks to her for sharing her personal and literary perspectives and her memories of the times that have so profoundly affected her life. Many of my initial questions have been answered, but there is a lingering sense of mystery in the questions that went unanswered or unasked. I remain intrigued, and anxiously await new encounters in her future books.

Readers will note that I discuss here only Guy's books that are of primary interest to young adults. I have not included her book for adults, *A Measure of Time,* or her book for young children, *Paris, Peewee, and Big Dog.*

Finally, heartfelt thanks to my family and friends (editors included) whose faith in me was reflected in their actions.

Rosa Guy
Photograph by LeRoy Henderson.

Chronology

1914   Marcus Garvey organizes Universal Negro Improvement Association (UNIA) in Jamaica.

1917   UNIA chapter organized in Harlem.

1925–?   Rosa Cuthbert born in Trinidad, third child of Henry and Audrey Cuthbert. Her parents emigrate to the United States.

1927   Marcus Garvey deported from United States.

1929   UNIA International meets in Kingston, Jamaica.

1932   Rosa and her sister, Ameze, join their parents in New York City.

ca. 1933   Girls live with Garveyite cousin during their mother's illness.

ca. 1934   Mother dies. Rosa and Ameze return to Harlem and their father.

ca. 1937   Father dies.

ca. 1939   Leaves school to take care of her sister and works in brassiere factory in the garment district.

1941   Marries Warner Guy. Studies with the American Negro Theater while her husband is away in the service.

1942   Son, Warner, born.

1945   Moves with her husband and son to Connecticut.

1950   Returns to New York after breakup of marriage. Joins

Committee for the Negro in the Arts and meets John Killens.

1951 Begins Harlem Writers Guild with Killens.

1954 One-act play, *Venetian Blind,* produced at the Topical Theatre in New York.

1960 Two short stories, her first published work, appear in C. L. R. James's newspaper in Trinidad.

1960 Meets Maya Angelou at Harlem Writers Guild meeting.

1961 Organizes march on the United Nations to protest Lumumba's death. Meets Malcolm X.

1962 Goes to Haiti after death of former husband; begins work on novel.

1965 Malcolm X assassinated.

1966 *Bird at My Window.*

1968 Martin Luther King assassinated. Goes south to research youth reaction to the events of the sixties.

1970 *Children of Longing.*

1973 *The Friends.*

1976 *Ruby.*

1978 *Edith Jackson.*

1979 *The Disappearance.*

1981 *Mirror of Her Own. Mother Crocodile.*

1983 *New Guys around the Block. A Measure of Time.* Documentary based on *The Friends* produced in England by Thames television.

1984 *Paris, Peewee, and Big Dog* published in England.

1985 *My Love, My Love; or, The Peasant Girl. Paris, Peewee, and Big Dog* issued in the United States.

1. Beginnings

My life in the West Indies, of course, had a profound influence
on me. It made me into the type of person I imagine that I am
today. The calypso, the carnival, the religion that permeated
our life—the Catholic religion—superstitions, voodoo, the
zombies, the djuins, all of these frightening aspects of life that
combine the lack of reality with the myth coming over from
Africa, had a genuine effect on me. But it was an effect that I
knew nothing about, didn't realize played an important part
in my life until much later when I was writing. But they
made for an interesting background . . . something that I
could call back on, something that I could hold onto as I went
into a new life, a new environment. Something that gave me
a stake, I suppose one would say. So that when I say I am
West Indian, I have all of these little things—all of that
broad background—that makes up the thinking, the searching of a person when art becomes relevant.

Rosa Guy

Rosa Guy is an islander at heart; she feels a certain sense of
freedom in an island with its views stretching unimpeded to the
horizon. Although years and miles separate her from her birth-
place, the island retains a special place in her life. It is both a
real locale and a metaphor for home, warmth, tradition, values,
and roots.

She was born on the island of Trinidad, which might easily be
the model for the fictional island she has described as the "jewel

1

of the Antilles" (*My Love, My Love,* 1). References to the island abound in her work. It is a comforting memory for young Phylissia Cathy in *The Friends,* an abused and lonely adolescent growing up in New York's strange and impersonal environment. She recalls how different things had been there: "On the island everybody cared about everything. And there was nothing wrong about being alone either. . . . I remembered how much I used to like to be alone" (14). For Ruby Cathy, in *Ruby,* the island is the place to which she turns for direction: "Unhappiness, nostalgia, sadness and loneliness conspired, forcing her thoughts away from classes, school. She longed to be on the roof of the highest building in New York—to communicate with the day, to feel a closeness to the island that would give her direction" (28).

For Guy's characters, the island is always present, its memory providing them with a respite from the cold, impersonal city in which they live, invoking an image of nature and growth against the concrete and stagnation they see around them.

Child of the Island

The warmth and security of Guy's island beginnings are centered on her family. Facts about her birth and early background are a source of contention, however. She was the second of two daughters born to Henry and Audrey Cuthbert. Two dates of birth appear in standard biographical sources: September 1925[1] and September 1928.[2] Guy declines to verify either one. Specifics about her early years in Trinidad being limited, reliable impressions, rather than facts, are all that can be determined about her life until she arrived in the United States at age seven or eight— impressions garnered from the reflections of West Indian culture and tradition in her work.

Trinidadian mores and traditions and the natural beauty of the island were integral parts of her early years. The warm temperatures, luxuriant vegetation, and spectacular physical features provided young Rosa a splendid playground. Here she absorbed the unique culture of the island—an admixture of African, Spanish, French, English, and East Indian cultures in varying degrees. The family and the Roman Catholic church, permeated with the vestiges of African culture that survived the slave system, were the dominant institutions in Rosa's community. Friends and kin were important, and both the church and social traditions emphasized respect for elders.

The oral tradition is strong in Trinidad, and storytelling and verbal ability highly prized. That Guy sees herself as a contemporary storyteller is consistent with that tradition. This emphasis on verbal proficiency is evidenced in the rhythm of everyday Trinidadian speech. Guy reflects a special feel for language in her work and confesses her delight in the way Trinidadians make up language as they go along. Years later, when she was living in Harlem, the verbal abilities of the youngsters "playing the dozens" (a semiserious game of verbal putdowns) and the imaginative hustlers' language of her stepmother and her friends reminded her of the richly imaginative speech of her home island. Even today, her own speech is graced by the rhythm, the spontaneous repetition, and the rich imagery rooted in the oral traditions of Trinidad.

The sense of warmth, security, and acceptance Guy remembers from her childhood was a natural extension of growing up in a close-knit community in a land where people of color constitute a majority of the population. Harmony with nature, the strength of the extended family, and strong traditional and religious values provided both substance and direction for young Rosa. She saw positive reflections of herself in those around her and experienced a reassuring sense of stability as a consequence.

The Emigration of Her Parents

A longstanding part of the social framework of Trinidad, high unemployment levels have made emigration an attractive alternative for each new generation of residents. Guy's parents were among the thousands who emigrated from Trinidad to New York City to find work during the years of World War I. Part of the great migration begun during the war to replace workers who had gone off to fight, immigrants like the Cuthberts were initially welcomed. There were jobs in America, and the Cuthberts, like many before them, left their children behind with relatives, sending for them at a later date when a job and housing had been secured. The economic promise of the new land seemed a prize worth the temporary separation from family and home.

As the immigrant ranks swelled, the newcomers became political forces to be contended with in large industrial cities. White workers, convinced that blacks would lower wages and take away jobs and housing, feared them. Newcomers like the Cuthberts, arriving in the Harlem of the 1920s, found a large, self-contained immigrant community—a ghetto created by the exclusion of blacks from white residential areas. Yet the enforced isolation provided a refuge of sorts in an alien land. Straining at the seams with the continuous influx of newcomers, black institutions and culture flourished.

The Immigrants' Harlem

The sense of community and mutual protection the immigrants found in the ghettos solidified the growing reputation of these communities. Harlem became a mecca for blacks from both the South and the West Indies. But the Harlem the newcomers found offered both promise and peril. Formerly the province of wealthy whites, Harlem was now a teeming community of new arrivals replacing other minorities who had come before them. All such newcomers encountered abuse, but West Indians faced a twofold prejudice. Because of their race they were consigned to Harlem by the larger white community, but because of their different language and customs they often met with resentment from the black Americans with whom they lived.

On the other hand, the pressure-cooker effect of this crowded mixture of black life-styles also produced the magic of the Harlem Renaissance and a spirit of black nationalism that has had an enduring effect upon black Americans. Those of West Indian heritage were especially active in black cultural, political, and entrepreneurial activities. A Jamaican, Marcus Garvey, was one of the most popular leaders of the time, capturing the hearts and minds of the black urban masses. He was to have an important influence on Rosa Guy.

Garvey, sometimes called "Black Moses," was a journalist by trade and a dynamic orator. He had developed his speaking skills through frequent participation in the street debates that were a popular pastime in Kingston, Jamaica, where he began his journalism career. Out of his experience in labor organizing and publishing in the West Indies, his personal encounters with racism, and his reading of the works of Americans like Booker T. Washington grew the idea of organizing a group to unite all people of color. He founded the Universal Negro Improvement Association (UNIA) in Jamaica in 1914. During a visit to the United States, he assumed leadership of the Harlem UNIA chapter, having found that blacks in the United States were a receptive audience for his views.

The UNIA platform of economic betterment, promotion of black self-worth, rehabilitation of the image of the black woman, and support of the brotherhood of all blacks had an arresting effect upon the masses of black Americans. They were daily faced with segregation and discrimination in housing, employment, and education; constant denigration; and frequent episodes of racial violence throughout the country. Garvey's organization, based in Harlem, expanded throughout the West Indies and into Central and South America. The establishment of the *Negro World,* a weekly newspaper and UNIA house organ, increased Garvey's popularity. The *Negro World,* unchallenged among publications of the period for its black literary coverage, published both established and aspiring black American writers, as well as those from Africa, Canada, and the Caribbean. A weekly readership of about 200,000 in its peak years, 1920–22, attested to the hunger of its readers for black literature and political news.[3]

The spirit of racial pride that lay at the bottom of Garvey's practical programs—the founding of a chain of black-owned groceries, restaurants, laundries, and other businesses—and his flamboyant style appealed to the majority of blacks, even those who disagreed with his ultimate goal of emigration to Africa. The pageantry of uniformed members of the African Legion and Black Cross nurses marching under the red, black, and green UNIA banner was a welcome sight in Harlem, dramatically embodying the spirit of racial pride that Garvey sought to promote.

Although he was a pariah among the black elite of the twenties—those who formed the core of the cultural flowering called the Harlem Renaissance—his sense of race consciousness and pride was often echoed in their work. Langston Hughes is a noteworthy example. In an article written for the *Nation* in 1921, "The Negro and the Racial Mountain," Hughes voiced the frustrations of a small cadre of young black writers and stated the tenets of their new perspective:

> Without going outside of his race, there is sufficient matter to furnish a black artist with a lifetime of creative work. . . . An artist must be free to choose what he does; certainly, but he must also never be afraid to do what he might choose. . . . We younger Negro artists who create now intend to express our darkskinned selves without fear or shame. If white people are pleased, we are glad. If they are not, it doesn't matter. We know we are beautiful. And ugly too. The tom-tom cries and the tom-tom laughs. If colored people are pleased we are glad. If they are not their displeasure doesn't matter either. We build our temples for tomorrow, strong as we know how and we stand on top of the mountain; free within ourselves.[4]

The cultural renaissance of the twenties made the name Harlem internationally known, and it endured until the last years of the decade. The demise of the renaissance accompanied the rapidly deteriorating social conditions that culminated with the stock-market crash of 1929 and the beginning of the Great Depression.

It was sometime during this period that Rosa and her sister arrived in New York to join their parents, although the specific date is unknown. An *Essence* magazine article, based on an interview with Guy, indicates that her parents sent for her and her older sister, Ameze, when Rosa was eight years old.[5] Writer Maya

Angelou in her autobiographical novel, *The Heart of a Woman,* states that Guy "had lived in New York since she was seven years old."[6] Still another source cites the year of her arrival in the United States as 1932, but does not give her age.[7] Asked about these dates, Guy laughingly says, "I don't tell the year."

Whatever the date of their arrival, young Rosa and her sister were in no way prepared for their new life in depression-ridden Harlem. They had been transported to a community that was the polar opposite of all they had previously known. Trinidad was warm; Harlem was cold. Trinidad was a haven of friends and kin; Harlem was white against black, black American against West Indian, and all against the poor. Harlem was big, impersonal, and uncaring—not close, not secure, not *home.*

Among the sketchy facts about these early years, two pivotal experiences stand out. Within a short time after the family had been reunited, Mrs. Cuthbert became ill. And second, because of her illness, Rosa and her sister were sent to live with cousins in the Bronx who were followers of the charismatic Garvey. Thus, in the home of her cousins, Rosa was first exposed to Garvey's nationalistic philosophy. Guy remembers this period fondly: "That's where I did my first little poem at the Garvey meeting and stood up at the corner and listened to the Black Garveyites." She attributes the activism of her later years (which she sees as simply an expression of human concern) and her passion for language to the Garveyite influences in her girlhood. It gave her a consciousness that other people did not seem to share. "I had an awareness of Africa that other people didn't have. I had an awarenesss of language because my cousin spoke so many different languages." This early exposure to a politically and intellectually stimulating environment served Guy well in the years ahead, offering her a firm educational background upon which to build.

Although she recalls that Garvey was not in the States when she arrived there, his paper, the *Negro World,* was published until 1933, a year after her estimated arrival. This period and the activities in her cousins' household must have offered some respite from the generally negative nature of her new environment and her fears for her mother's health. But her time there was short; it ended with her mother's death about two years after the family had been reunited.

The lives of Rosa and her sister were dramatically changed by their mother's death and their new life with their father. Returning to live at home, the girls were cut off from the Garvey movement, which Guy insists never really died out in New York. (Some members of the Garvey movement, often called nationalists by the press, stayed around until the beginning of the African independence movements in the early 1960s, offering Malcolm X a following upon which to build.) No Garveyite, Rosa's father had goals that were no less well defined. Guy describes him as an aspiring capitalist: "He was here to make money and he wanted to make money." That left little time for Rosa and her sister. The deepening depression finally shattered her father's capitalist aspirations, however.

Even before the stock-market crash, more than half of the nation's black banks had failed, a sign of the catastrophe yet to come.[8] The very nature of black enterprises (largely oriented toward recreational, retail, and service businesses) made them easy prey as the devastated economy took its toll. The depression was a downward spiral that began with the failure of businesses and banks and the loss of vast fortunes by wealthy whites and ultimately resulted in unemployment for millions of workers. Without jobs there was no money for spending or saving. By 1935 the full impact of the depression was chillingly evident—breadlines, homelessness, and miserably overcrowded living conditions were rampant. Black unemployment figures in some northern urban centers reached as high as 60 percent,[9] and even as late as 1937, the figure was nearly 40 percent.[10]

Shortly after her mother's death, Rosa's father became one of the depression's casualties. He was remarried briefly to a flamboyant transplanted southerner whom Guy would later write about in the novel *A Measure of Time*, but his economic fortunes never took a turn for the better. His second marriage over and his dreams for the future shattered, he died several years later.

Orphans in New York

Guy's reticence about the years that followed—the orphan years—indicates the difficulty of the period for the two young girls coping without parental support. Reflecting on the years of her youth, she remembers being an outsider. "The whole [experience] of always being on the outside looking in, in a way formed me," she says. The sisters' experience with life in institutions and foster homes after their parents' deaths shaped Guy's perspective on life. Although she provides no specifics, her simple, emotion-filled statement—"I've been in a home; I've seen things"—speaks volumes. She believes that family relationships and childhood experiences condition our interpretation of life. "Being an orphan at a young age," she says, "had to affect my personality, the way I see things, the way I absorb things." The sensitivity with which she would later write about young adolescents confronting parental loss and institutional life reflects these pivotal experiences in her own life.

As orphans, the two girls were forced to grow up quickly. Looking back, Guy remembers her sister as a special anchor in her life, and the two were always very close. As the elder, Ameze always took care of Rosa, but at age fourteen, when her sister became ill, young Rosa assumed the caretaker role. Quitting school, she went to work in a brassiere factory in the garment district. Although she had been forced to drop out, she nevertheless remembers experiencing a sense of profound freedom. She was no longer a victim of the limited social space and expectations allowed a West Indian girl by adults at home, at school, and in the community at large. At fourteen years of age, she was a free and working "adult."

Moreover, she was finished with the abuse from intolerant classmates. Only years later, after the publication of her first book, did Guy realize how much she had been affected by her childhood experiences with her peers. Confronting in her own writing how thoroughly she had internalized the pain and resentment of her youthful tormentors, she could only "regret that there had been no books yet written, no guidelines from caring adults . . . [to] guide us over the deep but narrow ravines dividing us."[11]

A Life among Artists

By age sixteen, Rosa was both wife and worker. She had met and married Warner Guy and continued to work in the factory while he was away in the army. But she was also a seeker, looking for some way to express herself, to share her insights into the life she saw around her. Because of the isolation of her earlier years she gravitated toward artists. "I sort of went out of my way to meet them," she says, feeling a kinship with these people who seemed never fully part of society. At the factory Guy met a young actor who introduced her to the American Negro Theatre, (ANT), where she was to find many kindred spirits.

The dramatic proving ground for an array of celebrated black theater professionals, the ANT was founded in 1940 by playwright Abe Hill and actor Frederick O'Neal. Its primary objective was to demonstrate the talent and capability of black actors and to destroy the stereotypical images of blacks in the performing arts. The theater was at its height when Guy discovered it. Its production of *Anna Lucasta* went on to become a smash Broadway success in 1944, and fellow theater members who became widely acclaimed later include Sidney Poitier, Ruby Dee, Harry Belafonte, and Alice Childress. The birth of a son, Warner, in 1942 cast Guy in a new role—mother—but did not dampen her interest in the theatre. Although Guy never performed in any ANT productions, she studied acting with both Osceola Archer and Abe Hill. Before she had fully developed her skills, however, her husband returned from the army and the family moved to Connecticut. In Connecticut Guy threw herself into the roles of wife and mother, "working at it," she says, until the relationship faltered.

Guy returned to New York in 1950 after the marriage ended

and once again sought out the artistic community. She learned that the once vibrant American Negro Theatre had died out during her years in Connecticut; in its place, however, she found the Committee for the Negro in the Arts. The committee had been formed in 1947, and it shared the aims of its predecessor, the ANT: widening opportunities for blacks in the theater and the elimination of racial stereotypes in the arts. Guy was also impressed with the politics of the committee members, feeling that "they had a broad understanding of what was happening in the world in terms of the exploitation of black countries and the relationship of such exploitation to the plight of blacks in the United States."[12] An umbrella organization, it included members from all areas of the arts. Although she had been drawn to the committee because of her interest in acting, her involvement eventually led her to write.

The civil rights movement, in the 1950s, began in earnest, but blacks in the theater found themselves faced with a paradox. The early battles against discrimination waged by organizations like the ANT resulted in an unusual backlash. White playwrights and producers, who became sensitive to the racism inherent in the roles previously reserved for blacks, such as servants and comical characters, stopped including such stereotypes in their plays. But they failed to replace these roles with other parts for blacks or to consider blacks for the many diverse roles available in any production; consequently blacks were in danger of being eliminated from the stage completely. Protests from the Committee for the Negro in the Arts and other groups had only minimal results.

Guy's personal response to this situation was a creative one. She began work on a one-act play to help remedy the dearth of material available for black actors. She wrote the play with the specific objective of ensuring herself a part in it. The successful one-act play, *Venetian Blinds,* was staged in a small off-off-Broadway house called the Topical Theatre. She got her part. But, she recalls, "it was a one-shot deal and after this play I started writing short stories."

The Harlem Writers Guild

Coping with the experiences of life as one of the urban poor and observing the relationships of the people and events she encountered had forged in Guy a compelling desire to express her understanding of the world in which she lived. Acting offered her an initial outlet, and joining an organization like the Committee for the Negro in the Arts provided a support group of people with similar aims. Among its members were people who were also interested in writing. One of them was John Killens. He had been part of the CNA's disbanded writer's group, but, along with other former members including Walter Christmas and John Clarke, he had stayed in touch with the organization. Guy gravitated to these people whose ideas and hopes were similar to her own. "What we wanted to do was to have a group that really projected the life, the style, the dialogue, the type of writing, [the] expression that could only come from the black experience in the United States, and in my situation, of course, the U.S. and the West Indies. So together with these people we formed a workshop—a workshop called the Harlem Writers Guild."

Formed in 1951, the workshop was a support group and a critical forum for writers. They read their works to the group, listened to criticism, and then "rewrote and rewrote and rewrote." Guy vividly recalls the workshop's early years, especially the hardships of its members who had to accommodate the urge to write with the need to support their families. "All of us were workers, doing some other type of work. I was working in a brassiere factory making brassieres. And every evening I had to come home to write. Mornings, I had a son to get dressed and get off to school, and then I'd go to work. I did this for a period of years. And it took quite a few years because at the time publishers were not necessarily interested in black writings, nor in our concept of what writing should be."

Killens was the motivating force for the group. The publication of his first novel, *Youngblood,* while he was "reading" in the workshop was an inspiration to the young writers coming through. There were many: Paule Marshall, Audre Lorde, Douglas Turner

Ward, Lonnie Elder, Maya Angelou, among others. Guy estimates that between 1950 and 1970 more than half of the black writers in the country were associated with the workshop. She remembers Killens as being especially influential in her life, encouraging her to stick to it in her writing. Guy did stay with it despite her curtailed education, the demands of her job, and the responsibilities of single parenting. She was talented and determined to be more than just Rosa Guy, factory worker. It was a challenge, but the choice was hers, "whether . . . to act or write or do something! It was a driving force in me. It was a driving force in that orphan, out there on the streets . . . who needed something through which to express herself, through which to become a full-bodied person."

The Harlem Writers Guild was an important part of Guy's education. Its workshop provided some of the training she had missed when her formal education had been interrupted. In later years she pursued tutorial studies with Viola Brothers Shaw and attended New York University. Its standards were rigorous, she says, so rigorous that her first book was not published until 1966, sixteen years after the guild was formed. During those years she had been writing, learning, perfecting her craft.

Guy experimented with a variety of genres over the years. From her first venture into the artistic world as an actress, through her play, short stories, and novels years later, she struggled to find a voice and a form for that voice—a vehicle through which she could "express herself," through which she could "become a full-bodied person."

2. The Making of a Writer

The 1960s, for all its traumas, was one of the most beautiful periods in American history. Only yesterday? So it seems
to those of us who lived through it. Television sets were in the
homes but had not yet taken over the responsibility of parents. Drugs on the streets had not yet changed youth gangs,
fighting over turf, into addicts, robbing everybody's turf.

Young people, strong in their beliefs, came out in numbers
to follow Martin Luther King, Jr. They marched, sang, pro-
fessed unity, a dedication to justice and human dignity for all.
Black and white students, understanding the dehumanizing
effect of poverty, shouted slogans, "Black Power," "Black is
Beautiful," into Black communities to arouse the youth to
their potential.

What an outpouring of literature—about Blacks, about
Spanish, about Indians, Chinese. Americans suddenly wanted
to know the kind of world they were a part of. They were ea-
ger to do something for the good of that world, help cure its
ills.

Rosa Guy, "All about Caring,"

During her early years with the Harlem Writers Guild workshop Guy worked at writing short stories. Two of them, her first
published works, appeared separately in 1960. On a trip home to
Trinidad that year she had met historian-journalist, C. L. R. James,
then the editor of a Trinidadian newspaper. Guy showed James
some of her stories, and he published two in his newspaper. Even

in these early efforts, Guy's work reflected her bicultural heritage. One story, "The Carnival," was based on a Trinidad tradition. The other, as Guy remembers, derived from her experiences in the brassiere factory in New York. The short stories were never published in America, and though Guy herself has tried to find them, there are apparently no surviving copies.

The Civil Rights Movement and African Independence

Returning to the United States in the latter part of 1960, Guy found New York City a center of action. The Harlem Writers Guild was abuzz with activity, its workshops a gathering place for the cream of black artists and those who aspired to write. Because the United Nations was located in New York, the city was center stage for many dramatic events during the 60s: African countries moved for independence, concern over the arms race intensified, and the birth of the civil rights movement in a bus boycott in Montgomery, Alabama attracted worldwide attention.

It was an exciting time. Guy had many friends and acquaintances in both the arts and the African diplomatic communities, and so she stayed abreast of rapidly changing events. The ferment was intercontinental. The link between Africa and black America was demonstrated daily as the chains of oppression were cast off by people in Africa and North America. The activities of Martin Luther King, Jr., and the Southern Christian Leadership Conference (SCLC) inspired the African freedom fighters; black Americans in turn watched with pride as African countries claimed independence.

These events were of central importance to Guy and members of the Harlem Writers Guild. After writing, politics was their favorite topic, and at any given meeting someone would have news of a visiting dignitary or an impending event. One such meeting during Fidel Castro's 1960 visit to the United Nations, for example, culminated with the writers' adjourning to join in a welcoming party at the Teresa Hotel for the Castro entourage.[1] Given the close community of the Harlem Writers Guild, it was all but impossible for individuals active in the arts or politics not to know at least one of the guild's members or some of their many acquaintances. All were not only interested but actively involved in civil rights and African independence efforts.

Guy's long friendship with black novelist Maya Angelou began at a guild meeting in 1960. Angelou had been encouraged to leave California and come to New York to study in the Harlem Writers Guild by guild cofounder, John Killens. The two women became fast friends. Angelou worked as a northern coordinator for SCLC in the 1960s and was also involved in African independence efforts. After her marriage to an African diplomat, she lived and worked in several countries there. As for Guy, Angelou recalls that "Rosa was writing every day, coping with her rambunctious family, being courted by handsome African diplomats and working in a factory to pay her rent."[2]

The two often initiated social involvement projects for their cadre of friends. In her novel *The Heart of a Woman,* Angelou recounts the founding of a women's action group by herself, Guy, and actor Abbey Lincoln. The Cultural Association for Women of African Heritage (CAWAH), formed to support black civil rights groups, brought together dancers, teachers, singers, writers, and musicians. The charter, drawn up by writer Sara Wright, pledged the group to raise money for, promote, and publicize efforts to further a just society and "to perform dance concerts, song fests, fashion shows and general protest marches."[3]

One of their first and most memorable efforts was a protest of the death of African leader Patrice Lumumba. Guy had met with Lumumba only months before, and although the news of his death was generally withheld, she learned of it through a Congolese diplomat. Angry and hurt by the loss of such a strong leader, Guy and Angelou induced CAWAH to organize a protest at the UN on the day the death was to be announced. The January 1961 protest, which had been envisioned as a silent one in the UN Assembly Hall by CAWAH members and associates, quickly turned into a massive demonstration. It was disclaimed by many black leaders and called a riot by the media. It also indirectly set the stage for Guy's first meeting with black leader Malcolm X.

Malcolm, who came to national prominence in the sixties, reminded some observers of Marcus Garvey with his powerful oratorical ability and his emphasis on black worth. Undaunted by criticism of the UN demonstration, Guy approached Malcolm to enlist his support for the cause of African independence. She was impressed by his verbal prowess and was disappointed to find that he was totally involved with Elijah Muhammad and the Muslim cause and did not choose to join her coalition. Although this first meeting was unsuccessful, their paths would often cross before his tragic death. They had much in common—among other things, an exposure to Garveyism in their youth. The murder of Malcolm's father, in fact, is said by some to have been a result of his involvement with the Garvey movement in the South.

As the sixties continued, marches, pray-ins, sit-ins, riots, and assassinations convulsed the United States. The unrest and violence the South had experienced from the inception of the civil rights movement moved north in 1963. Open confrontations between blacks and whites erupted in Cambridge, Maryland, that year, and school boycotts and rent strikes plagued Chicago, Boston, New York, and Cleveland. The tone and intensity of the movement changed, as the protests and the backlash escalated. The Sixteenth Street Baptist Church in Birmingham, Alabama, was bombed during Sunday school hour in 1963. Freedom Summer workers James Chaney, Andrew Goodman, and Michael Schwerner were brutally murdered in Philadelphia, Mississippi, in 1964. The next year, during the Selma, Alabama, march, Viola Liuzzo was shot to death. A summer uprising in Harlem in 1964 set the stage for five years of what would be called "long, hot summers"—violent outbursts in black communities across the country. One of the worst was the August 1965 riot in Watts, a large black community in Los Angeles. A year later, Student Nonviolent Coordinating Committee member Stokely Carmichael's declaration of "Black Power" rang across the southern countryside and echoed in the nation's consciousness.

A New Black Renaissance and Private Pain

Hand in hand with the unrest, however, came a level of creative energy that had not been attained in the black community since the 1920s. It was a second black renaissance, especially in literature. Its rebirth is almost perfectly aligned with the shift in perspective from the early years of the civil rights movement with its stress on nonviolence to the years marked by the articulation of the black power concept. John Killens had manifested a distinctive black awareness in his works as early as 1954, but now the tides of social change that swept the country led other black writers to acknowledge that the time had come for a new vision in their works. More than anyone else, Imamu Baraka, first known as Leroi Jones, is acknowledged as the synthesizer of this new literary perspective, which gave a unified philosophical base to black writers. Baraka has described the important features of the movement thus:

> Erupting out of New York, the Black Arts literary stance came to be taken up by black writers all over the country. . . . Just as the Harlem Renaissance literature had reflected the lives and struggles of the people, so the young Afro-American writers who were part of the Black Arts movement of the 1960s consciously wanted to create a contemporary Black Art that was (1) BLACK (an art that utilized the forms and content of Black life); (2) revolutionary (an art that would transform America, that would help Black people transform it); (3) mass-oriented (a literature that would reach and educate the masses of Black people); and (4) oral (a literature that would be spoken and public, not an academic literature conceived and received and read in deadly silence).[4]

The influence of this vision was widespread, even among those who did not actively embrace the movement.

The controversial literary perspective was indeed not embraced by all black writers, but whatever their sentiments, all gained from the new outlook. The debate over art as functional or "for art's sake" was at last largely laid to rest. Looking to themselves—to their own cultural traditions—black writers found parallels in the traditions of African art in which all creations serve some cultural function. Moreover, increasing numbers of black artists accepted the task of re-creating and thus transforming the black experience, finding it neither creatively limiting not antithetical to considerations of form.

Although not a proponent of the black arts movement, Guy was influenced by the tone it set in the literary community and the interest it provoked in the country at large. She has described the sixties, despite the traumatic events, as "one of the most beautiful periods in American history." America was being explored again. There was an outpouring of literature about blacks, Native Americans, Hispanics, and Asian Americans. "Literature was brought to a new high"("Caring," 195).

Guy was more affected, however, by the escalating pace and intensity of events taking place. The violence that marked the period was not only societal but personal as well. Recalling the murder of her former husband, Warner, Guy insists that "all of it was a part of the whole." The kind of conditions that kept blacks oppressed led not only to public unrest but caused individuals to "act and react to each other violently." The traumatic effect of violence in Guy's life had its impact on her work. After the murder of her husband in 1962, she left the United States for Haiti. There, she says, "the trauma of [her] husband's death and an earlier moment of violence in the life of a childhood friend" impelled her to start work on what would become her first published novel.

The assassination of Malcolm X in 1965 was the culminating event in this "awful period" in Guy's personal life. Guy feels strongly that her life was "intertwined with Malcolm's". She had kept abreast of his activities since their first meeting and found herself near the scene at the time of his murder. She had seen him some weeks earlier and had counseled him against an upcoming speaking engagement at the Audubon Ballroom. He failed to heed her, however. She recalls being in Presbyterian hospital when Malcolm was killed. "The hospital was right across the street from the Audubon Ballroom and I could look out of the window and see this crowd while I'm listening to the radio and hearing about his being shot down. I saw when they brought him across and I was just about out of my mind, up on the sixth floor someplace and knowing that he was downstairs, and not knowing if he was dead." It was an experience, she said, that "seemed really fateful. . . . I'd probably never be in the hospital again for the longest time in life—and there I was right on the scene at that particular moment. And I always felt very strange about it. There I am, the person looking in; I'm always there."

The loss of Malcolm was shattering. It was the coda to a theme played out again and again on the streets of Harlem—brilliance snuffed out, or in Guy's words, "channeled into a life of crime and self-destruction by the crushing confinement of prejudice and poverty"("Caring," 193).

Bird at My Window

After Malcolm's assassination on 1 February 1965, Guy resumed work on her novel. In 1966, after years of writing, the book, *Bird at My Window,* was published. Wade Williams, its protagonist, exemplified for Guy the tragically shortened lives of her husband and her childhood friend. Worn down and eventually made destructive to himself and others by the forces of poverty and racism Wade kills his own sister. Such senseless loss of lives and destruction of youthful genius became a theme Guy would often embrace in her writing. The book was dedicated to "Malcolm—the pure gold salvaged from the gutter of the ghettos in which we live—and to all the Wades that were not."

Bird was received with mixed reviews. Brooks Johnson, in the *Negro Digest,* praised the book for its evocation of Harlem and its treatment of the sociological and psychological forces that cause "the gradual amoralization of a black man in Harlem," but he also noted that "unlikely and false-sounding words came out of very unlikely mouths."[5] Noted black writer and critic Saunders Redding, speaking at a black writers conference in June 1966, charged that "preoccupation with repossessing a heritage had led to distortion of values and reality . . . making heroes out of heels."[6] He named Guy's *Bird,* as well as works by James Baldwin,

John A. Williams, and Chester Himes as culprits. Generally, however, the critics agreed that Guy was a writer to be watched.

The continuing social turbulence that marked the years after publication of *Bird* acted as a catalyst for Guy. Her interests and experiences conjoined to produce the mature vision she would later express in works of special interest to young people.

Children of Longing

The "long, hot summers" reached a fever pitch with the assassination of Dr. Martin Luther King, Jr., in 1968, and Guy, like so many others during this period, decided to go south for the first time. "I was so affected by the death of these two leaders [Malcolm X, King]; I could say three, because Lumumba's death certainly had affected me. And just the fact that no sooner than you start building up heroes—they get knocked down like that!" It was frustration and anger, then, that moved her to action. "I felt that when Dr. King died I just had to go. So I went to my editor at that time [Greg Armstrong at Bantam], and I said 'I want to find out what the young people are thinking.' "

Guy thereupon set out to discover how these powerful events were affecting the lives and attitudes of youths not just in New York or Mississippi but across the country. The result of her investigations was a nonfiction book, *Children of Longing,* a collection of essays written by youths and transcriptions of interviews, all united by Guy's highly personal commentary. A book clearly capturing the mood and prevailing outlook of the nation's black youth, *Children of Longing* proved to be an emotional and literary watershed for Guy. Its creation signaled a convergence of the concerns of Rosa Guy the writer and Rosa Guy the black activist, whose viewpoint would become even more evident in her later works.

The book is unlike her other work in that it marked a transition point in her development. Although its purpose was an investigation of the influence of the social upheaval of the sixties on black youths, it was in many ways a by-product of that turbulence.

Its form and its unifying idea were representative of the spirit of the time in which it was written.

In the course of her extensive travels gathering material for *Children,* she went "to Black high schools and colleges in urban and rural areas, to writers workshops, the cottonfield and the ghettos seeking answers from young Black people between the ages of 13 and 23."[7] She was sobered by what she saw. In much of the South she encountered fear and resentment of outsiders and admits that she was "scared to death." An urban dweller for most of her life, she felt that her experiences in the rural South broadened her vision.

But the hopes, anxieties, and struggles of the young people she met everywhere also struck responsive chords in her memory. Their questions and concerns were basically the same no matter what the location or the circumstances. They were the questions of youth coming of age. More than fifteen years later she affirmed the significance of these experiences and her deeply personal concerns about youth. "I write about people, all people—white, black, anyone I meet . . . but I do dwell quite a bit on the lives of young adults, black young adults, coming up in the United States. Because coming up in this industrial society is a very hard road for anyone to travel."

The writings and the interview material she collected in her travels provided a plentiful supply of themes and characters that would serve as raw material for her later works. Some examples from essays in *Children* are illustrative. The street-wise personality of sixteen-year-old Leslie Kroup was echoed in the character of Imamu Jones in Guy's fourth novel, *The Disappearance.* Twenty-three-year-old Paris Warner's description of the day his long-absent father—who, Paris had boasted, was an Arizona rancher—came around and "messed up [his] lies" formed the kernel of one of the most wrenching scenes in Guy's novel *Edith Jackson.* Characters like Al Stacy, perhaps the closest thing to a role model that Imamu Jones finds on the streets of Harlem in *The Disappearance,* and Imamu Jones himself, bear names more than coincidentally resembling those of real individuals like Al Stacy Hayes, and

Imamu Baraka (Leroi Jones) who were part of the black revolt of the sixties. The writing produced by these young people was in itself special, for the book showcases the talent of two prospective young writers Nikki Giovanni and Eleonora Tate. But even among the less articulate, the heightened consciousness and desire for change so frequently reflected in their writing were compelling. Although their lives were often precarious, Guy found few destroyed and destructive Wade Williamses among these young people. They had, as one young essayist succinctly put it, "seen the world as it really was" and had chosen to change it. It was a point of view, a vision of life, that complemented Guy's own outlook and contributed to the evolution of her personal literary vision.

Acknowledgment of the realities of the past and present, self-affirmation, and individual and group insistence on change are at the heart of *Children,* as well as of Guy's own philosophy. She has said, "You know, the cliché is that a good writer is supposed to show the way. But to so many people there's such hopelessness and unless we start realizing their hopelessness how do we point the way?"[8] In *Children,* Guy brought her readers face to face with the devastating realities with which so many young people must struggle. But she demonstrated through their words a new perspective that spoke of pride and hope, and of a belief in cooperative efforts for social change.

As an outsider herself, Guy could present their world with a special sensitivity and compassion. Having grown up black, female, West Indian, and an orphan, she is deeply empathetic and committed to others cast in the role of outsider. Her orphan's experience has given her a unique angle of vision, and her experience as a minority figure, by virtue of both race and cultural background, adds yet another dimension, enhancing her observational skills.

Aware of both the similarities and the differences in the human condition, she takes a global view in which everything is "part of the whole." The measure of her characters is taken in terms that reach to the roots of her own experiences, but the questions framed are universally relevant: What are the realities of our lives? How do we see ourselves and what do we aspire to become? What are the consequences of our choices? What can we do to make a difference in our lives and in the world?

She says of her writing: "I do believe that I'm trying to say that we live in one world and it's a damn small world and we have to care for each other. We have to be concerned about that world." She maintains that there is no such thing as individuality or self-determination that cannot reach out in love, concern, and caring for others: "The survival of one of us depends upon all of us." It is this underlying judgment that shapes her special way of seeing, aligning the distinct lenses of Rosa Guy black woman, West Indian, and orphan into a unified literary vision with many facets.

3. Independent Artist

I'm a storyteller. I write about people. I want my readers to know people, to laugh with people, to be angry with people, to despair of people, and to have hope. More than that, I want my readers to know just a little bit more, to care just a little bit more, when they put down a book of mine.

Rosa Guy, *Boston Globe* Book Fair Symposium, November 1984

Rosa Guy writes with the conviction that art can transform life. This vision, a product of her African heritage, her Garveyite background, and her experiences during the sixties, has been the foundation of her later work. In the years since the publication of *Children of Longing,* she has published seven novels and one picture book translation, earning a reputation for the creation of works of complexity and emotional richness. The experiences and emotions of adolescence have remained among her special concerns. Her knowledge of the urban scene and her ability to recreate the experience of coming of age in a city environment distinguish her work of the seventies and early eighties.

Essays of the Seventies

Essays captured Guy's interest after publication of *Children of Longing* in 1970. It was in this format that she chose to express her incisive knowledge of Harlem and her concerns for the young people growing up there. In the article "Black Perspective: On Harlem's State of Mind" (*New York Times Magazine,* April 16, 1972) Guy explored for the reader the scenes and sentiments of America's premiere black community. She traced Harlem's evolution from "capital of the Black World" to "dying city." After interviewing residents, she recorded their views on the deterioration, crime, drugs, injustices, and indignities in their daily lives, expressing both their frustrations and their hopes. She focused particularly on "the poor young dropouts who came out of the harsh realities of the crumbling cities but did not succumb to the drug culture." Although the form was different, the interview methodology and the issues raised in the essay were similar to those of *Children of Longing.* The introductory paragraph sounded a note that would recur, in some fashion, in all her future work: the blight of the slum must be combated or "the sickness that it creates will one day consume us all."

Still another essay was on her mind when Guy arrived in Algeria to visit with her friends Roget and Jean Genou. With *Children* and articles like "The Black Perspective" behind her, she planned to write now about the orphans of New York. The subject, of course, was personally meaningful to her and was something she felt the public knew little about. Its four characters, Phylissia, Edith, Ruby, and a Puerto Rican youngster named Sylvia, were real people she had known when she and her sister lived in an orphans' home. "I always must have wanted to write about them," she says, and although it took a while, "they came back."

The essay was critiqued by Guy's friends in Algeria and, on her return to the United States, by workshop members. Although Guy disagreed with the workshop criticisms, she remembered the enthusiasm of an Algerian friend who loved Edith Jackson, and Roget Genou's comment that the piece "was more a storylike thing" than an essay. After much thought she was convinced that Genou had been correct. When she finally showed the essay to her editor at Bantam, Greg Armstrong, it was with the simple declaration, "Greg, I think I want to make some novels."

Almost compelled by the "storylike thing" her characters had to express, Guy began work on her second novel. This was the beginning of what would become her acclaimed trilogy—*The Friends, Ruby,* and *Edith Jackson.* Comments Guy, "I took the two characters Phylissia and Edith—and I left Sylvia, who's a very interesting character—and made *The Friends.* And then *Ruby*—who was very special to me—and then the other side of Phylissia, of course, was *Edith Jackson.*" After many years of writing in varying forms, she had finally found her true voice in the novel.

The treatment of the growth to womanhood of the three young black women in these novels has marked the trilogy as among Guy's finest work. Internationally praised, it has been translated into many languages. Two of the novels, *The Friends* and *Edith Jackson,* appear on the standard list of required reading for the British school system.

Major Works

The deterioration of the inner cities during the unfolding years of the seventies touched Guy's work in much the same way the turbulent sixties had molded her earlier works. Just as her *New York Times Magazine* essay factually traced the movement of Harlem from its original boundaries and condition through the creeping decay in the seventies, her novels created a fictional history of the Harlem community. The trilogy, which covers approximately a three-year time span, chronicles the deteriorating conditions in Harlem as the girls are growing up. The three books were followed in 1979 by *The Disappearance,* a novel in which the growing devastation of the community is palpable. The dying Harlem community is, indeed, one of the protagonist's strongest adversaries. The publication of *Mirror of Her Own* and *Mother Crocodile* in 1981 represented departures from Guy's previous work, the first sign of an impending change of direction in her writing. *Mother Crocodile,* on which she collaborated with the illustrator, John Steptoe, is Guy's translation of a Senegalese folktale. *Mirror,* her only work that does not focus on a black protagonist, is a coming-of-age story set in a bedroom community "on the Connecticut side" of New York. Highlighting political and social issues such as economic colonialism, pan-Africanism, and racial and class prejudice, the novel and the picture book are the first of Guy's works not set in Harlem and/or focused primarily on the black experience.

A banner year in her career was 1983. *Ruby* was reissued, *Edith Jackson* appeared in paperback for the first time, and two new novels were published: *A Measure of Time,* a biographical novel based on the life of Guy's stepmother as well as an evocative chronicle of Harlem, and *New Guys around the Block.* The latter book continues the story of Imamu Jones begun in *The Disappearance,* graphically portraying the death of the old Harlem while subtly hinting at Guy's turn toward her island heritage.

In 1985, Holt, Rinehart and Winston published *My Love, My Love; or The Peasant Girl.* A tender West Indian love story based on Hans Christian Andersen's "The Little Mermaid," the book draws on Guy's West Indian background. Rich with the lore and language of the Caribbean, it also expresses her concern about the social and economic conditions of the people on many of the islands. It is a book she has always wanted to write. She views it not only as an opportunity "to give another part of myself" but as a chance to reflect on the contemporary situation at a distance—to redefine relationships and perhaps gain a new perspective on the world in which we live.

Primary Themes

Guy's concern over the deterioration of the inner cities in the aftermath of the sixties is a focal point of her works produced before the eighties. In these novels she inducts her readers into the state of mind and existence of the ghetto. Harlem is the setting, but it is representative, in some respects, of every inner city; it is a setting with the impact of a living character. Home and community on the one hand, it is an antagonist of monumental proportions on the other.

Guy is not unique in her use of this setting, but her highly realistic detailing of the social dynamics and the evolution of the ghetto as a social antagonist sets her apart from other writers using predominantly inner-city settings. Her distinction rests in her consistently multidimensional, evolutionary treatment reflecting broad universal themes. Hers is a symbolic Harlem, which is also real. The dilapidation and destruction she chronicles throughout the five Harlem novels are not imaginary; the emotional and experiential truths of the novels arise out of her ability to re-create the essence of people's lives. In describing influences on the evolution of her work, she has targeted the violence in American culture, personally dramatized for her by her husband's violent death and experiences in the lives of friends. But Garveyism and finally the movements of the sixties forced a national acknowledgment of the roots of much of this violence in historical and socioeconomic conditions. Guy's post–*Bird at My Window* novels, including her young adult works, reflect the strong sense of social affirmation she felt in these movements, as well as her concern over conditions in the cities in their aftermath.

The facts of the settings and situations in her work are as real and tough, humorous or touching, as the language the characters use to describe it. Her accurate and detailed portraits of inner-city life turn upon expressive imagery and distinctive use of figurative language. The sociohistorical and emotional reality of the inner city is reproduced through her use of the characteristic idiom of urban black and West Indian Americans. The humor and irony often encompassed in this richly expressive vernacular gives her work a special vitality and naturalness.

Violence and fear are ravagers of the ghetto community's talents and spirit. And so they are part of her characters' lives—monstrous conditions raising very personal questions about survival. From Guy's perspective, however, violence and fear are also universal issues shaping human interactions in nations, cities, suburbs, and towns, challenging individual and community alike.

Viewing the domestic situation as only one part of a larger picture, she raises global questions relevant to us all. What is the relationship of the United States to the Third World countries?

What are our responsibilities to the world? What are the responsibilities of youth? "How," Guy asks, "do we fit into a totally
mechanized society where people are going to the moon, planning
to use space as a military stage, while we are fastened and held
onto dreams that were dreamt twenty years ago?"

These concerns are an integral part of the judgment that informs her work and makes it as contemporary and relevant as
the ever-changing events of our world. "The age of innocence is
gone," she says, "done away with by the television."[1] And so she
writes to give young people "the broadest kind of understanding,"
for "the future of our world depends upon the kind of understanding which has to start with the young."

The issues and conflicts Guy explores are neither age- nor cul-
ture-bound. Choice and responsibility have a crucial place in her
personal and literary vision. She admits that she sometimes finds
it difficult to read some books classified as "young adult" because
they do not deal with young people as young *adults*. "They make
them a different breed of people, and I don't feel they are a different breed of people," she says. "I think they have responsibility. . . . I think they have to start life understanding this."
She is sensitive to the particular challenges of young people coming of age, however. Indeed her novels are most often set in a
problem-solving or discovery mode, effectively reflecting the search
for self that is such an integral part of coming of age.

Novels that treat the personal growth and development of an
individual during youth have a long tradition. The bildungsroman, or "novel of education," can be traced back to its German
prototype, Goethe's *Wilhelm Meister's Apprenticeship*, published
in 1795. Although for years the bildungsroman featured protagonists who were white and male, the 1960s and 1970s saw changes
in the tradition as black males and then women began to chronicle
their own growth experiences. Rosa Guy's work has contributed
to the reshaping of this tradition. Critic Geta LeSeur has suggested that novelists write these books either to rediscover childhood roots or to expose conditions that have limited or impeded
their growth and development. She has also identified several
characteristics that West Indian and Afro-American bildungs-

romans share: "By comparing and contrasting the stories about boys growing up with those about girls growing up, both in the West Indies and the U.S., some interesting conclusions can be drawn. In all these novels race, color and class have an impact on the child's consciousness."[2]

Guy's work, particularly her trilogy, exemplifies the characteristics LeSeur has identified. Her work is distinctive, in fact, because it targets the growth of young women—from a woman's perspective—by blending cultural rediscovery and the exploration of sociohistorical issues. It is thus not only a part of the evolving female bildungsroman tradition but a comparative novel of education that considers the development of young women from different social and cultural backgrounds. In *The Disappearance* and *New Guys,* Guy illuminates some aspects of the development of young black males in the inner city with the same sensitivity and insight she has exhibited in her treatment of young women.

The outsider's viewpoint informs everything she writes; her life has so shaped her consciousness. Growing up black, female, West Indian, and orphaned, and consequently many times removed from the mainstream of majority culture, she empathizes with the outsider. She has a special affinity for the "new" girl, the kid who talks, dresses, or thinks differently, the inner-city kid negotiating outside home turf, and all those who most struggle to shape a life in the face of overwhelming odds.

The orphan is the ultimate outsider in her works, facing many developmental challenges without the benefits of family support. The contrast between the orphan and the family is clearly evident in her characterizations of Phylissia Cathy and Edith Jackson in *The Friends* and *Edith Jackson* and the life-style differences between the all-but-abandoned Imamu Jones and the Aimsley family in *The Disappearance*. Guy sensitively and realistically acknowledges the developmental perils and the prospects associated with both the orphan and the family experience, but emphasizes that we all—parents and teens alike—have choices to make, responsibilities to assume.

"I believe that life is before any teenager," she has written. "I try to leave all my characters with the hope that they can change

their future—that they have the right to change their future;
that they have the right to question parents; that they have the
right to make decisions based on moral values."[3] Guy's use of
"moral values" here does not mean, however, that her books express a certain set system of morality. In the body of her work,
the only consistently declared values are love and responsibility.
Indeed, in contrasting the life-style of the inner-city community
with other communities, the concepts of morality versus immo-
rality, acceptable versus unacceptable behavior, and right versus
wrong are examined. Motive and environment often raise tough
questions about ethical judgments. Guy provides no answers, establishing instead new, more critical ways of looking at these
concepts.

Rosa Guy is a writer not easily labeled, nor does she embrace
labels happily. She finds her peers among the writers who draw
on everyday life as a source of their art. "The things that happen
in day-to-day life in the black world, among black children, black
women and black men, capture my attention. . . . some incident
in the newspaper; something that happened to someone I know;
some tear I see in the face of a woman or child. All of these things
can start me working . . . everything in me moving forward to
do a piece of work."

Although she has had no declared role models in her writing
career, her reading interests are revealing. She greatly enjoys
European writers Victor Hugo and Gustave Flaubert. *Independent People* by Nobel Prize winner Halldor Laxness and *Jean
Christophe,* Romain Rolland's three-volume series in the bildungsroman tradition, are favorite novels. She considers them
more emotional models than role models, however. "I like all these
people," she says, "I like the feel of independent search . . . but
I find them all unique." She considers Richard Wright and Theo-
dore Dreiser two of America's great writers. She is impressed by
the more contemporary American writers as well: "Alice Walker
is good. Audre Lorde as a poet is excellent, and Toni Morrison—
spectacular."

From Flaubert to Rolland to Walker, the writing of each of
these authors conveys a strong sociohistorical sense, although

their themes and styles vary. Stylistically, perhaps the most direct line of artistic tradition for Guy can be drawn from the naturalist writers among her selections: Flaubert, Dreiser, and Wright. Guy's more hopeful treatment sets her apart from them, however. Only her first novel, *Bird at My Window,* seems to be drawn in the strictly naturalistic tradition.

Although she has been most often described as writing from the black and female perspective, even this label seems, for her, a bit too precise. "Long before feminism came in I was by myself. And long before the Black is Beautiful thing came in, I was a part of my cousin's household where everyone was talking about the Garvey movement. So that I find that, yes, I'm black and a woman, and I write from my perspective of being black and a woman, but not from somebody else's idea of it." In the final analysis, she defies labels. She is an independent artist, her writing distinctively personal, but strongly expressive of the issues and dilemmas of the times.

4. The Trilogy

Tiptoeing my way through the casualties of poverty in the
ghettos—an orphan in New York, ostracized for those traits
which being West Indian and Catholic had etched into my
personality—wasn't easy. I shall never forget the day I
walked, cringing, the length of a snowbound street and not
one snowball was hurled at my head. I knew I was grown up:
I believed myself immune from those influences molding the
lives of the Americans among whom I lived.

Rubbish, of course. I realized that when I looked through
the galleys of my soon-to-be published first book. . . . I had
internalized all their pain, their resentment—to the snow-
balls hurled relentlessly at my head, and firecrackers at my
feet—as I ducked and dodged my way through adolescence.
But I never looked back in hate—but with a kind of sadness,
a regret that there had been no books yet written, no guidelines from caring adults who might have made a difference,
guiding us over the deep but narrow ravines dividing us.

Rosa Guy, "All about Caring"

By virtue of both popularity and critical acclaim, Guy's trilogy
is the work upon which her reputation is based. Set in Harlem
during the turbulent years of the sixties and seventies, the trilogy
encompasses the central years of adolescence of Ruby and Phylissia Cathy and their friend Edith Jackson. Rather than following
a year-by-year progression, however, Guy focuses each of the three
novels through the eyes and experiences of one of the young women,
chronicling that individual's growth through a particular period

34

of time. Self-discovery is the conjoining theme, and although the structures of the three novels vary, Guy's attention to the cycle of the seasons, the characters' chronological growth across time, the evolution of Harlem, and the continuing relationship among the young women supports a unifying sense of growth and continuity in the books as a unit. Emotionally, although not literally, autobiographical, each book is as powerful individually as the trilogy as a whole.

Guy's unique holistic vision makes the trilogy a perfect form for her exploration. This format allows her to focus intensely on three major themes highlighting growth and self-development as seen through the experiences of the three young women: reconciliation-with-self (working through the reflection that society gives of oneself to a comfortable and realistic image of self and circumstances); reconciliation-with-another (establishing constructive nonfamilial relationships); and reconciliation-with-the-world (making choices and accepting responsibilities in the world).[1] Each book is an independent unit, however the connections between them make them three parts of a larger story. Her bringing the characters together again as the final book, *Edith Jackson,* ends leaves the reader with a vision of the three young women and where they are in their journey. It also reinforces the sense of the trilogy as a single story exploring the ongoing process of growth.

Lost innocence, courage, choice, and responsibility are recurring concepts throughout. Imposed images of acceptability (light skin, "good" hair, "decent" family) are sources of conflict, sometimes threats, in the development process. The bonds between women (sister to sister; older woman to younger woman, friend to friend) are a special kind of communion that Guy explores. The special challenges that confront the outsider are also graphically revealed.

The Friends

Published in 1973, *The Friends* is Guy's most critically praised work. It is a richly complex examination of a young girl's coming of age and the evolution of a special friendship. Phylissia Cathy and Edith Jackson are the friends of the title, two teenagers who come to share a strong friendship after a particularly stormy beginning. Culture, class, and language separate the girls like the ocean that separates the places of their birth. Fifteen-year-old Edith Jackson is Harlem born and bred. She is scruffy, bold, all-but-parentless, and poor. By contrast, fourteen-year-old island-born Phylissia, the protagonist, is bright, proud, and well cared for, but struggling to survive her new home in Harlem, her oppressive West Indian father, and her status as an outsider. Each is in need of a friend, but family, class, and Phylissia's insecurities dictate against it.

The friendship is played out in the heart of Harlem. A social pecking order reigns here, and as the immigrant newcomer, Phylissia is near the bottom. She is the target of ongoing abuse by classmates—led by the "big-breasted" Beulah—who despises her because she is different: prim, proper, West Indian, and academically prepared. She is rebuffed by her neighbor Marian and other children of Harlem's doctors and lawyers, who find neither her academic strengths nor her reserved behavior compensation for the fact that she "talks funny," is plain, and apparently is not as well off as they. But she is befriended by Edith, the shabbiest student in the class—one of the "ragamuffins" with whom her father has forbidden her to associate, below even Phylissia in Harlem's pecking order. Phylissia initially rejects Edith's offer of friendship—Phylissia's only such offer—simply because of Edith's very evident poverty.

This apparently doomed relationship is saved, however, by Phylissia's need for Edith, "the one girl she could use," to protect her from her hostile classmates who tease, taunt, and physically attack her. Thus Phylissia finally turns to Edith as a last resort.

Their fragile and essentially one-sided relationship begun, Edith shares all of New York with newcomer Phylissia, including shoplifted candy and "free" subway rides. She also shares her family—four younger sisters, a brother, and her broken father—with whom she lives in a shabby one-room walk-up. Phylissia, on the other hand, shares only stories of her "beautiful mother,"

her "glamorous sister," and her "ogre of a father with his fabulous restaurant," because she is too embarrassed by Edith's poverty and too afraid of her father's reaction to bring Edith home to meet them.

This sham friendship begun in the spring develops over the course of the summer. It is not an idyllic summer—Edith's father disappears and Phylissia's mother becomes ill—but the two girls share their hardships, secrets, and good times. The experiences forge a special bond between them. Edith has become Phylissia's secret friend, her best and only friend, although Phylissia continues to scorn Edith privately for her ragamuffin status.

Disaster results when Phylissia finally brings Edith home. Phylissia, who has camouflaged her ambivalent attitudes toward her friend throughout their summer together, launches a vicious, although indirect, verbal attack upon her friend, brutally humiliating her in front of the Cathys. The friendship shattered, Phylissia is left alone. The loss of Edith marks the beginning of a cycle of loss. Her mother's illness worsens and she dies. Phylissia's always distant relationship with her father deteriorates even further. The final third of the novel deals with Phylissia's lone struggle with guilt, grief, her father, and a developing sense of herself.

Guy compellingly captures the powerful forces of race, sex, and class that are at work in the girls' lives: race and sex uniting them in shared experiences, class driving them apart. Guy parallels the two young women in many ways. She has noted that they are fictional counterparts: Phylissia representing the family, and Edith, the orphan's experience. Their experiences as young girls growing up create a special bond between them, but their cultural and class differences reveal them in counterpoint. Guy uses contrast powerfully here, enhancing our sense of both young women, their relationship, and the forces that affect them.

Sisters in color, both girls suffer abuse because of their color. This conflict is a complex phenomenon for Phylissia especially. Both girls encounter the rebuffs of the color- and class-conscious children of Harlem's black professionals and of their teacher. Their racist white teacher, Ms. Lass, having taunted one of the quietest girls in the room about the oil in her hair, finally turns her racist assault upon the whole class declaring, "You come to school like pigs! Greasy, oily, filthy, pigs!" But Phylissia also confronts this conflict at home. Her father, she is aware, prefers "light-skinned women" and considers her ugly because she is plain and brown. She feels set apart because of her "plainness" in a "good-looking family." These interlocking conflicts are new to her; on the island her plainness did not matter, and racial shame such as she has been made to feel at school was not part of her upbringing.

True sisters also by virtue of their sex, the girls are tied into certain narrow role expectations. Poverty-stricken Edith is a catch-as-catch-can student destined for a life of domestic work. Phylissia, on the other hand, is cowed by her class-conscious, sexist, hypocritical West Indian father who demands that she be a prim, proper young lady and a good student and housekeeper while assuming that she will be sly, lascivious, lazy, and rude. Vacillating between overprotectiveness and distrust, his solution is to confine his daughters to the house when they are not at school.

Phylissia's family's background and expectations are also a source of isolation. Because she talks and behaves differently, she is verbally and physically abused and under pressure to conform to the accepted behavioral code. Since in physical appearance she is indistinguishable from her black American classmates, the differences in her language and behavior seem all the more unacceptable to them. And unlike her pretty sister, Ruby, her problems are not ameliorated by her looks, which to all except Edith, are unacceptable.

Yet class is a wedge driving the friends apart. Calvin, Phylissia's father, disdains those living in poverty. He prides himself upon not being like the poor black Americans he warns his daughters against:

> "You think I bring you to this man's country and set you down in good surroundings so you can make friends of these little ragamuffins. Just let me catch you with that girl again. And not only she, but any other one that looks like she. See what happens to that fast little tail of yours. It will be so hot with fire that you will pray for the gates of hell!" (63)

The irony that in a riot the police make no distinction between him and other blacks—swinging their nightsticks on West Indian and black American alike—is lost on him.

Phylissia is her father's daughter in this respect. Accepting her father's and society's standards of beauty and worth, she salves her personal hurt over rejection with a fantasy built around her father's braggadocio and ideas from stories she has read. She becomes the rejecter rather than the rejected. She initially rejects Edith and then uses her, while longing for the friendship of "round, brown, pretty" Marion with the "two long, long braids." But even when a true bond develops out of her sham friendship with Edith, her biases continue to surface. When the seriousness of her mother's illness compels her to seek Edith's help and counsel, her traitorous thoughts reveal her true feelings:

> I found that as much as I appreciated her, was glad to see her, I was still uncomfortable sitting next to her on the bus. . . . I had forgotten how shabby she looked. I kept telling myself that perhaps it was because I was dressed so much differently— but then of course the reason I had never invited Edith home was because she was so "shabby." (100)

Although friendship and family relationships are both important themes in *The Friends,* self-reconciliation is the central focus here. The three-part structure of the novel hinges naturally around three broad blocks of action: the development of the unlikely friendship, the enactment of Phylissia's personal protective fantasy, and the process of self-revelation. Each part serves a distinctive function but is seamlessly woven into the whole.

The first-person perspective gives us an immediate, intimate sense of the protagonist, Phylissia. Her every thought and emotion are revealed to us. She is our source of information about people and events in her world, which we get, of course, with her particular biases. Guy richly and economically builds upon this sense of intimacy between reader and protagonist to set the stage for events to come. In chapters 3 and 4 of part 1, she subtly establishes a basis for the tensions Phylissia experiences at home and at school in her immigrant background, while contrasting her world with that of Edith. She also artfully uses dialogue and action to create a more rounded view of characters and family dynamics.

Guy's handling of dialogue is special. She is as adept at capturing Edith's brassy street lingo as at rendering the Cathy family's rhythmic West Indian speech. Most important, however, she uses dialogue to reveal two characters—Mrs. Cathy and a family friend, Mr. Charles—as objective commentators against which Phylissia's perspective can be balanced. The shape of future conflict is foreshadowed in both content and the presentation of the conversation. In reasoned voices Mrs. Cathy and Mr. Charles discuss Phylissia's problems at school while Phylissia attempts to follow the intertwining dialogue. She strains to hear the voices of her mother and Mr. Charles over the loud, materialistic, and bigoted arguments with which her father is haranguing his cousin Frank. The presentation is almost theatrical, creating a powerful tableau through the content and juxtaposition of the dialogue:

> Mother: "Children can be cruel."
> I heard Mr. Charles answer: "Unhappily yes. Children are by far the most cruel of animals. . . ."
> Loud in the background Calvin: "He made a smart man and he made a fool!"
> I strained to give my full attention to Mr. Charles: "animals imitate their elders . . ." Cousin Frank in the background: "I just want to know what category he put you in, Calvin. . . ."
> Mr. Charles: " . . . animals are checked by instinct. But children must move past instinct to reason. . . ."
> Calvin: " . . . but you make joke, man. . . . You must see the money I make. . . . Two years in this country I opened up my first restaurant. . . ."
> Mr. Charles: "But at her age, children are still in a state of confusion. . . ."
> Calvin: "I'll open another and another. . . . I ain't like these damn fool black people. . . ." (28)

The technique subtly but dramatically furthers the unfolding plot by revealing character and setting an emotional tone for the novel. The result is a kind of four-part exchange. Calvin's blustery, emotional interjections seem to challenge the concerned and rational observations of Mrs. Cathy and Mr. Charles. The entire episode as seen from Phylissia's view gives a feel of the "state of confusion" Mr. Charles targeted as a part of the growth experience. It is also especially effective in conveying a sense of Calvin Cathy's character and the general family dynamics.

In Phylissia's brutal attack upon Edith, however, character is shown through action. Unaware of her own motivation, Phylissia lashes out at her sister for her calm and cordial acceptance of Edith, making it clear in her attack how much she disdains "the poor and dirty [who] went around with socks filled with holes and runover shoes." She is joined in the attack by her father. Arriving home unexpectedly, he verbally abuses Edith and orders her out of his home. Guy captures the parallel attitudes of father and daughter not only in the hostile, defensive dialogue but in the similarity of mannerisms as well. Guy describes Phylissia in her anger as "biting down on [her] jaws so that the skin rippled over them" (107). In the wrenching scene in which Calvin Cathy is coerced by his wife into an acknowledgment of the doctor's prognosis that she is dying, Calvin's reactions are strikingly similar. Crying out his agony, he "wanted now to fall, to hold onto something for support; instead he bit down so hard that the skin rippled over his jaws" (89).

Calvin Cathy is consistently depicted as a bold and blustery character given to braggadocio. Yet Guy sketches his background lightly, choosing to let his words and actions, and the views of others, tell his story. Once again it is Mrs. Cathy who provides the balancing view of Calvin Cathy. After his humiliation of Edith, his wife's reminder that there had once been a time when he, like Edith, did not "go with the furniture" in a "well-to-do" home is all the more telling. The sense all along that Calvin's bouts of overstatement are tolerated—even understood by his family and friends—suddenly fits. Although Calvin does not change, he is a more sympathetic character. Guy's method of characterization gives a strong sense of the deep-rooted insecurity that shapes his behavior and cements his self-image.

Throughout the novel, the sensible voices of Mrs. Cathy and

Mr. Charles offer us a more objective view of people and events, subtly focusing us on the central issues. Taking Phylissia to task after Edith's humiliation, Mrs. Cathy acknowledges her own culpability in the making of that shattering event. She also captures Guy's perspective on some of the problems of parenthood.

> If I had not been so caught up with all of my problems—my fears—I might have been able to see . . . what you were going through. . . . I never allowed myself to see that living in the same household with such a person as your father, it was natural that you copy some of his ways. . . . today was the first time I allowed myself to see that the things we love and accept, the things we value, make us parents our children's problems. (110)

She voices as well the challenge of responsibility that Guy sees as a part of growing out of the innocence of childhood into maturity. Even after her death, a spirit—which is by all evidence that of Mrs. Cathy—haunts Phylissia's sleep, prodding her toward that all-important revelation of her own character and responsibility.

The seasonal symbolism in *The Friends* does double duty as a measure of the girls' developing friendship and an objective correlative to Phylissia's changing emotional state. The friendship begun in spring is shattered in the late fall leading into winter. Mrs. Cathy dies shortly thereafter. That winter is, for Phylissia, a time of silent struggle—with grief, physical sickness, and the sickness of guilt that has been her mother's unusual legacy. Phylissia also struggles with her father. Fear of him has kept her from going to her friend during the long dark months of that winter. But she has also discovered that he is fallible. He has unjustly humiliated Ruby, frightening away the young man she is interested in because of a harmless good-night kiss. Since that time the girls have been all but imprisoned in the apartment. Phylissia, who in her innocence has always thought her father was right, cannot understand how he could be so wrong.

With this questioning comes a growing sense that his powers as a parent are less binding upon her; the struggle becomes overt.

The fragile self-image, which she has measured against his yard-stick, and her sense of her own place in the world have come unanchored. Even her body is deceptive. It has begun to change.

> I was changing. I felt the change big in me. . . . I now hated
> school, hated people—everybody except Ruby. My thoughts were
> disordered. . . . since my illness I had developed rapidly. My
> breasts were fuller than Ruby's now, so were my legs and thighs.
> I had even grown an inch or two taller. (147–48)

It is this "new" Phylissia who steps into the spring with an urge to do "death-defying things." These include skipping school, staying out late, and meeting a boy in the park—a boy who finds her attractive—all in defiance of Calvin. The price of this new boldness is her father's determination to return the girls to the island. Phylissia is unperturbed by this. What she finds truly disturbing is her first visit to her father's "glamorous" restaurant, which turns out to be merely a local greasy spoon.

The reality of her father's restaurant is literally sickening for Phylissia, a distortion of what she had envisioned in her self-flattering fantasies. It is in the fevered disorder of her thoughts after visiting the restaurant that she finally comes to grips with how her own fairy tale image of herself, and her attempts to maintain it, had brought great pain to her friend.

> I had seen things the way I wanted them to be. I had wanted
> to be an unhappy princess with a cruel king of a father. I had
> wanted to be the daughter of the owner of a big restaurant.
> Perhaps it was because the kids in school had been so hard on
> me. I didn't know. But I had wanted to be rich, to live in luxury,
> so that I could feel superior to them—to people like Edith. . . .
> I was the fraud. (173)

In the newness of spring Phylissia has come full cycle. Facing her own false image, she sees her insecurities and cruelty. Fired by a need to go to her friend, she defies her father's orders not to leave the apartment. She finds Edith grieving over the death of her baby sister, Ellen, and facing confinement in the Institution (an orphanage) with her other sisters. For the first time, Phylissia truly commits herself to her friend, praising her for being there for her family and pledging to visit and write while she is in the Institution. All the while she is aware that the future of that friendship, and of her relationship with her father, depends on her ability to forge some degree of communication with him.

In a final confrontation Phylissia stands up for the friendship and makes an impassioned bid to be allowed to remain in New York instead of returning to the island. She also makes a plea for a new relationship with her father. The novel's ending embodies both pain and hope. Calvin Cathy's inability to respond with any warmth toward his daughter is painful. He can only manage to brusquely charge her to put her clothes away and straighten the room. The girls, however, are allowed to remain in Harlem with their father. Although his verbal response is painfully characteristic, his tacit response belies the unemotional image he exhibits. His decision to keep his daughters with him hints at some hope for change.

The distinctiveness of *The Friends* lies in the Cathy family's bicultural background and the effective contrasting and comparing of Phylissia's West Indian American growth experience with that of black American Edith. Set against the backdrop of Harlem it allows us a look at the dynamics of Harlem life—the variety of life-styles, the inter- and intraracial color barriers, the class and cultural separations, and the subtle and overt perils of poverty and fear. These interlocking conflicts and circumstances and the characters' unique outsider status are sources from which incidents arise almost organically. Their evolution and/or resolution are intricately tied to the growth and development of the protagonist.

As the first novel in the series of three involving the Cathy sisters and Edith Jackson, *The Friends* tells its own story while laying the emotional and experiential groundwork for the other two novels. A trail of clues throughout the book foreshadows the major issues and conflicts in the growth cycle on which the trilogy focuses. These clues are interwoven to structure the complex meaning of *The Friends* while highlighting the connecting thematic strand that unifies the three books: a young girl's growth

to womanhood. In *The Friends,* Cousin Frank's sarcastic response
to Calvin's rough treatment of Ruby's friend Orlando—"What you
want her to kiss? A girl?" (155)—ironically presages events in
Ruby. In the same context, Mr. Charles's calm insistence that
Ruby has arrived at the age when she can do as she pleases and
his call for Calvin to allow both girls "a broader life" also prepares
the reader for the central issues in *Ruby.* Similarly, the evolution
of Edith's life in *The Friends* from tough, street-smart schoolgirl
to drop-out-turned-domestic worker in order to ward off the Institution foretells the kind of self-eroding conflicts that Edith
confronts in the final novel, *Edith Jackson.*

The Friends is an emotionally intense novel charged with Guy's
memories of her own experiences as a West Indian child coming
of age in Harlem—proud of her roots yet attacked for them, bright
and spirited but frustrated by the limitations that her race and
her physical features put on her. The memories are fresh and real.
She vividly recalls the loneliness, the isolation, and the shame
"because in trying to be part of the gang I've been cruel." It is
perhaps this universal emotional truth that so effectively holds
the novel together, creating a work that touches the reader's own
memories of the pains and joys of growing up.

Ruby

While *The Friends* is the story of Phylissia Cathy's first tentative steps into adolescence, *Ruby* explores her elder sister Ruby's turbulent initiation into the sphere of courtship and love
relationships. Here, too, the Cathys' bicultural heritage shapes
itself as a larger-than-life obstacle in the growth cycle, the focus
shifting from Phylissia's early adolescent years to eighteen-year-
old Ruby's emerging adulthood. Breaking free of the family circle
to embrace new, independent relationships is a dilemma frequently targeted in young adult literature, but the conflicts surrounding breaking away from the family orbit are exacerbated
for Ruby Cathy by the loss of her mother, the isolation imposed
upon her by her tyrannical father, and her cultural differences.

Ruby, who needs to "find herself, a likeness to herself, a response to her needs, her age, an answer to her loneliness" (47), finds an unlikely answer in the person of her compelling, enigmatic, and elegant classmate, Daphne Dupre. Arrogant, self-centered, and sometimes harsh, Daphne is the catalyst for change in Ruby's life, reordering the constellation of important people in her universe.

Ruby's universe is small and lonely. Except for Consuela—an outsider like herself—her former school friends have rejected her. (The deference of both girls to their racist teacher, the result of cultural backgrounds mandating respect for elders, is interpreted as "Uncle Tom" behavior—an unforgivable sin.) Her sister is absorbed in books and writing letters to her friend Edith, while her father, preoccupied with work, takes time only to frighten off any young men who show an interest in her. Until Daphne enters her life, Ruby has felt alone except for a solitary oak, standing like a sentinel outside her window. In Daphne Ruby finds an answer to her loneliness—a new existence outside of the family sphere; a new name, Bronzie; and a special place, Daphne's red-lighted room. The friendship develops into love between the two girls. Ruby's father, however, is not a man who will accept or understand his daughter's need for Daphne.

When initial attempts to conceal the relationship fail, a tense emotional tug-of-war ensues between the demanding father and an equally demanding Daphne. Ruby is caught in the middle. The tug-of-war is initially fought with Calvin's subtle efforts to control Ruby's comings and goings and to limit the time she can devote to her new relationship on one hand, and Daphne's attempts to have Ruby spend time with her, on the other. But when a subterfuge designed to allow the girls an entire weekend together fails, the war escalates, and Calvin physically punishes Ruby. The episode only strengthens the forbidden romance, despite the disapproval of both Mr. Cathy and Mrs. Dupre.

Ultimately the relationship ends in the natural course of events. With the rapid approach of the close of the school year, Daphne's plans for college and the future collide with the teenage romance. Ruby, who has no plans that have not been built around Daphne, is devastated. In the cliff-hanging climax she attempts to commit suicide rather than face the end of the relationship. She is saved by her bewildered father who makes a naive but genuine effort to help her forget the shattered love affair.

Ruby generated no small amount of discussion, the controversy largely centering on the book's focus on a love affair between two young women. But the novel's meaning and distinctiveness lie not in any lesbian or bisexual overtones but in the uniqueness of the two young protagonists. Guy's concern in the novel is the development of the characters. Almost polar opposites by virtue of family backgrounds and experiences, they are briefly and explosively linked by their common need for love and acceptance. Although the conflict between family and lover is explored, Guy's real focus is on the growth and development of the two young women. Much has been made of Ruby's female lover, but the major conflict in the love relationship has little to do with Daphne's gender. The conflict on which Guy focuses this love story would exist no matter who, or what sex, Ruby's lover might be. For the problem arises out of the ages of the protagonists and their family relationships, cultural backgrounds, and unique personality traits.

The love relationship between the two young women is very much Guy's kind of plot structure. It is a reversal, a commonplace event turned about. But it is not a casually chosen structure. The romance between the two young women allows Guy to explore the growing need for nonfamilial relationships—one of the central developmental issues young people face—from a distinctively female point of view, looking especially at how family dynamics, cultural background, and individual personality traits influence development. Daphne's growth, although not the primary focus here, serves as a point of comparison in looking at the major developmental issues the two young women confront so differently.

From its emotionally charged beginning to Ruby's climactic suicide attempt, her feelings and emotions are the novel's central focus. In the opening scene, Guy paints Ruby's world in shades of gray, with only an occasional splash of color. The imagery sets the novel's tone but also establishes a firm groundwork for Guy's ongoing characterization of Ruby. In the evocative opening pas-

sage—"Loneliness like a vapor wafted from her bowels . . . slith-
ered along her throat . . . preventing its erupting into screams,
hysteria, torrents of tears" (1)—Ruby's emotional state is firmly
established. She is alone and lonely. The truth of her life in Harlem is captured in the scene she surveys from her window—Marion moving, Orlando passing her by:

> Friendships were like that in this country—fluid as water,
> fragile as those modern buildings which so often replaced the
> graceful, lovingly constructed old houses—quickly erected and
> as easily destroyed. . . . Ruby rested her gaze on the oak tree
> which grew like a sentinel outside her apartment . . . gnarled
> and determined, sparse but aggressively promising. . . . The
> day darkened. . . . Ruby was about to turn when she spied a
> pair of broad shoulders through the branches of the trees. . . .
> Ruby knew who it was. . . . *I used to like him but now I don't—*
> *I used to like him very much. But now I definitely don't.* (p.3–
> 5)

The tone is set, the character base laid, and the outline of impending conflict subtly sketched. Guy literally moves us through
the novel on Ruby's emotional swings. Page after page of the third-
person narrative is punctuated with Ruby's anxiety-filled reveries
and all-but-hysterical thoughts. Ruby even takes a degree of pride
in her theatrical flair for expressing her fear and anxieties: "I
feel so stupid . . . so stupid. . . . I didn't use to be . . . I didn't
. . . Oh God! . . . What am I to do? I am like a desolate island
in a stormy sea. . . . She liked that simile. 'A desolate island in
a stormy sea' " (35).

The symbolic use of the seasons of Ruby's sentinel tree under-
scores the passage of time as the eighteen-year-old moves into
the "broader life" that Mr. Charles envisioned for her in *The
Friends*. Her move outside the sphere of family into the world of
friends and love relationships is aptly set in the time of the buds
"swollen with impatience to leave although it was barely spring"
(4). The imagery Guy uses in these early pages subtly and effectively projects Ruby's sensitivity, her fragility, her lack of experience, and her need for someone.

Daphne, "of the smooth tan skin, large white teeth . . . black shoulder length hair, colorful silk shirts and tweeds" (15) is the catalyst for the new Ruby. Superior in all things, both physically and intellectually, she uses her gifts to her own ends, eschewing tradition and propriety and evoking reluctant admiration even from those who dislike her. Young, proud, and self-directed, she has been unalterably marked by her father's accidental death. She is obsessed with care, caution, intellect, and controlled instincts. She is adamant that she will, at all costs, avoid death on a "hummer" (a pointless accident) and remain always "cool, calm, collected, poised, sophisticated, refined," and, of course, intelligent.

Ruby's intellect and spirit blossom under Daphne's care and tutelage, but Calvin Cathy proves to be an equally powerful force in his daughter's life. In Calvin, Guy has created a fully consistent character. Towering over his family, both literally and figuratively, he keeps his daughters at arm's length from himself, yet allows them no space for other relationships. He threatens rather than talks; inspects rather than interacts; and suspects rather than respects his daughters. Yet loved by both girls, he is a powerful force in their lives.

Guy captures the delicate maneuvers of father and daughter in the smallest detail as they attempt to preserve some semblance of their old relationship—Ruby to preserve her privacy, and Calvin simply to maintain control. But the battle is joined from the time Calvin and Daphne first meet. The first half of the novel focuses on the emotional tug-of-war in which Ruby is caught. True to her theme, Guy evinces this battle of wills through its impact on Ruby.

Calvin spies and he plots, controlling his daughter indirectly at first. The impact of Calvin's implacable will is felt even in his absence. Ruby's anxiety is palpable. The ringing of the phone shatters one carefree Saturday afternoon spent at Daphne's apartment, triggering the specter of disapproving Calvin and spoiling the afternoon's fun. Ruby's anxieties about her father's disfavor cause the strong-willed Daphne to exert even more pressure: "What are we, prisoners? . . . Ruby Cathy, your step toward freedom was certainly limited. You must stop this nonsense! You are not a child. You must tell your father" (89). Guy infuses the treatment of this war for Ruby with some light touches, and the interactions of father and daughter are powerfully captured through Guy's deft use of dialogue. Both father and daughter are prone to hyperbole that is often both humorous and revealing. A burnt meal causes Calvin to declare hysterically, "Oh, Go-od! . . . You burning me house down. . . . I leave the house one minute next the place going up" (59).

The quips and antics of Phylissia also lighten the tension. Miss Effie is a minor character brought in by Calvin to supervise/spy on the girls. Her futile designs on Calvin infuriate Phylissia and prompt some of Phylissia's most creative and humorous verbal and tactical assaults. Guy also effectively uses Miss Effie's behavior as a seriocomic parallel to Ruby's fawning behavior toward Daphne. Foreshadowing the fate of Ruby, Miss Effie is summarily banished by Calvin when a nightgown, purposefully placed on Calvin's bed by Phylissia, convinces Calvin that Miss Effie is invading his house.

The depth and range of Ruby's emotions are effectively revealed throughout these early chapters. Guy keeps the tension drawn taut until the pivotal moment of Ruby's dramatic demonstration of compassion for her vitriolic teacher during a fire drill at school.

Guy's powerful description of the crippled teacher's unaided struggle to grasp her cane during the drill is masterfully done, capturing the seething cauldron of hate and racism that is part of her characters' lives while bringing all the tensions of the first part of the novel to a crescendo.

> No one moved. The teacher's torment mesmerized them. Even if there had been a fire, they could not have moved. Waiting to see her perish, they would have perished with her, so tightly did she bind them with her hatred. . . . For Ruby, it was the most painful moment she ever experienced, the most shameful. (101)

As Ruby affirms her instinctively caring nature and steps out of the line to help the tormented teacher, she forever seals her fate with her classmates and seems to doom her relationship with Daphne.

Relaxing the dramatic tension at last, Guy uses natural imagery to evoke the unwinding emotional tension, the sadness, the giving in to loss. Through the living room window Ruby can see her special tree,

> heavy with leaves . . . bent under the heavy rain, its fragrance pleasing, yet achingly nostalgic. . . . Everything happened so quickly. A short time ago, it had barely begun to bud. Was it so short a time? I hadn't known Daphne then . . . not really known her. . . . now . . . I feel for her so deeply. . . . I can no longer see her. (107)

Ironically, it is Ruby's demonstration of compassion that subtly changes Daphne, cementing rather than destroying the relationship as Ruby had feared

Throughout the novel, the third-person perspective allows the reader a kind of rounded, objective view of Ruby, but Guy artfully controls what we know and when we know it. She begins building toward the revelation of Ruby's true character early. Her imagery in descriptions of Ruby in part 1 hints that there is another side to her loving, compassionate nature. When Mr. Charles describes Ruby as a kitten needing lots of love and attention, her father differs with him: "Kitten? Is what you call it? Calvin scoffed. You mean cat, ain't you, Charles? You ever see a cat playing with a mouse? They play, they play . . . then all of a sudden . . . they hold and hold and they don't let go" (27).

More telling than the observations of unsympathetic Calvin, however, are Ruby's own thoughts. She remembers how she had attended her mother during her illness: she had "cared and cared . . . surrounded her with love," and had resented her mother's attentions to Phylissia on that last night before she died. This is a reflection of the darker side of Guy's vision at work, her ability to see the underside, the "grotesque," in commonplace events and actions. This other side of Ruby's nature is the key to a real understanding of her character, which emerges in the last half of the novel. Guy structures this revelation of character through the cumulative power of description joined by action, dialogue, and the careful handling of the device of space.

What Guy makes clear in imagery and action is that Ruby's need for validation through others is the compelling force in her life. Ruby's words to Daphne are illustrative: "I am blank, Daphne. Nothing is written on me until I feel for someone like I feel for you. When you leave I become blank again" (118). Ruby's statement is not simply an expression of love; it is an honest assertion of an operating dependency in all her relationships. Phylissia's sarcastic comparison of Ruby with Chaucer's constant Griselda is apropos (132). Love for Ruby consists less of sharing than of needing, and the need is endless. Rather than risk loss because of disagreement or disapproval, she gives, adjusts, accepts, defines herself in her relationships with others. The startling differences in the personalities of Daphne and Ruby enhance the impact of this revelation.

It is this dependency of Ruby's and, concomitantly, Daphne's singlemindedness about her future plans that spell inevitable doom for the relationship (rather than anything to do with Daphne's sex). It is ultimately a question of space—room in which to grow and change. Guy expresses this conflict both literally and figuratively. The love affair that began in Daphne's red-lighted room flourishes within small confines. The girls experience much happiness in the room guarded by the red light or behind the locked doors of Ruby's small room. But Ruby is not bold enough to allow the relationship to move beyond these small spaces.

The girls plot to spend one "beautiful, free weekend" together, safe from Calvin. He has reluctantly given his daughters permission to visit their friend Edith in Peekskill, thus providing the perfect cover. When Calvin discovers that Ruby has spent the holiday weekend with Daphne rather than chaperoning her sister on her trip to Peekskill, he publicly beats her. He struggles with anger and fear. Despite all his ploys—the "family dinners," Miss Effie, and his spying—he has been unable to command his daughter's complete loyalty, devotion, or obedience. He does not confront the full meaning of her disobedience—her womanhood and sexuality. Banishing her to her room, he unwittingly sends her into the sympathetic arms of Daphne.

It is Mrs. Dupre, Daphne's mother—concerned for her own daughter's safety given Calvin's volatile temper—who confronts the situation head on, expressing her disapproval of the relationship and effectively putting Daphne's room off-limits to the girls. Although she has played the part of ally in their efforts to delude Calvin, her own demeanor and, finally, her words challenge her daughter (and Ruby) to look honestly at the relationship: "If Ruby feels like putting up with [the situation] that is her business. She's old enough to make her own decisions. What makes you the great know-it-all? What makes you the one who must think for us all? To decide for us all?" (145). As the school year draws to a close, the girls confront Mrs. Dupre's challenge in their discussions-turned-arguments over personal plans and plans for the relationship.

Symbolically, the critical turn in the relationship takes place in Ruby's locked room. Guy displays the unique twists of her imagination as a surprise birthday celebration for Daphne in Ruby's bedroom collides, disastrously, with a similar celebration for Calvin taking place in the living room. By the time of the fateful birthday celebration, the locked door has, ironically, become a symbol of Daphne's presence. Even Phylissia has become conditioned to assume Daphne's presence behind the closed door: " 'Why else would the door be locked?' she asks," (154). And it is in this symbolic usage of the rooms that the problem with the relationship is graphically demonstrated.

The privacy, security, and respite from loneliness that the confined spaces of the girls' rooms have offered have, ironically, now become imprisoning, allowing neither the girls nor the relationship room for growth. Daphne's growth—her plans for college and the future—has not been matched by similar growth on Ruby's part. Ruby is unwilling or unable to risk her security for the space necessary to grow. On the night of the birthday parties, Ruby's lack of courage to grow is symbolized by her unwillingness to open her bedroom door and expose Daphne to her father and his guests. Her refusal to open the door dooms the relationship.

Guy's description of Daphne's escape down a sheet out of Ruby's bedroom window echoes the stages of development of the relationship: an initial tense tug-of-war, followed by an abrupt relaxation of tension:

> Ruby thrust Phylissia aside and with a quick movement caught the rapidly unwinding sheet, twisting so that it wound around her body in one turn. . . . Bracing her hands on the sides of the frame, . . . she stood as the sheet drew tighter, tighter around her waist. . . . Suddenly, inexplicably, the pulling stopped, the strain was gone. (162)

Daphne's close brush with death on a hummer spells the end of the relationship, except for the final declaration. We are prepared for the last climactic events of the novel by Ruby's escalating emotionality. Her mood and demeanor, indeed the circumstances leading to the novel's climax, are like a flashback to Ruby's lonely, emotional state in the novel's opening scene. The "flashback" is a reconstruction of the opening scene—the emotions (the loneliness, the loss, the denial), the imagery, even the narrative cadence—but in a compressed form: "Fear came rushing back. . . . Ruby pictured herself looking out her window at the lonely tree, the singular street, the disinterested passersby. She tasted the ashes of her love, thick on the back of her tongue. *How can I let her go? I shall never let her go*" (172).

Although Daphne is sometimes seen as an unsympathetic character, her brutality in ending the relationship is both in character and understandable in light of Ruby's resistance to confronting her own selfishness. Daphne's blunt declaration of the end of the relationship occurs, appropriately, in Ruby's *unlocked* room:

> You want to be loved. You need to be loved. You have to be loved—by everybody. . . . No one must escape your need for love. . . . we have had our time. . . . we have been good friends. We enjoyed each other. It is over. I want to live, and there is no life in clinging, pretending. (178)

Ruby's suicide attempt, the question of her future relationships, indeed the resolution of the novel have been controversial. Regina

Williams, in a lengthy review in *Interracial Books for Children Bulletin,* finds the novel full of "mixed messages." She is disturbed by Calvin's inviting Orlando to visit Ruby immediately after the suicide attempt; she feels it is just one element of the book's sexism. She further asserts that although Ruby's personality problems were the story's central element, they remain unresolved at the conclusion of the novel.[2] Williams is not impressed by *Ruby.*

The answers to Williams's criticisms can be found in a consideration of Guy's style and characterization. After preventing his daughter's suicide, Calvin's response, as demonstrated by his invitation to Orlando, is true to his nature. It is typically, simplistically, and—yes—sexistly Calvin. Yet his sending for Orlando has a positive side: it is tantamount to capitulation, to an acknowledgment that his suspiciousness and possessiveness were wrong. He is not sensitive enough to see that (as Williams points out) Ruby's unresolved problem is her dependency, but we can hope, as Ruby Dee has suggested, that Ruby will "find her way."[3] Ruby's response to Orlando's arrival—"maybe tomorrow"—is openended; she is not hurrying to fasten her dependency upon him. Time is required for Ruby to sort out the events of the past months, her own feelings and emotions. We can be certain that the relationship with Daphne has been central to Ruby's growth and development. Her thoughts clearly indicate this: Daphne "was so important to me . . . my life. . . . yet she said I was selfish, . . . selfish . . . selfish" (182). Guy makes it clear that the nature of Ruby's relationships in the future is purely a matter of her own personal development.

The same is true of Ruby's sexual orientation, which is equally a matter of personal development. As Judith Mitchell in an *Alan Review* article noted: "If one had to sum up Guy's attitude toward homosexuality from this story, one would conclude from the internal evidence that she believes the need to love and be loved is paramount. To assuage that hunger, young people may fall in love within or outside their own gender. What determines the success or failure of the relationships may have more to do with personality than with being male or female."[4]

The book has been described as "a very sensitive novel in which adolescent homosexuality is viewed as nothing so frightening, but perhaps just a way-step toward maturity."⁵ The concept of relationships of any kind as steps toward maturity is appealing and in line with the overall theme of the trilogy. In this respect it is intriguing to consider Guy's imagery in describing Daphne's room—Ruby's haven from her lonely, emotionally turbulent existence. The room is located down "a long darkened hallway from where she could see the sun lighting the drawn shades of the living room. [It is] before the living room at a corner where the hall turns sharply. [Inside there is a] second door, closed off by heavy-wine colored drapes, matching the drawn draperies at the window which obviously lead back into the L-shaped hall" (39). One would suppose that there are other rooms (relationships) along that long dark hallway leading to the sun-lit living room. The imagery is resonant with the sense of journey—through the darkness of innocence and inexperience toward the sun of maturity.

Edith Jackson

The culmination of Guy's trilogy is the novel *Edith Jackson.* Phylissia's devoted companion in *The Friends,* Edith takes center stage here. Although she has shared some of her important developmental years with the Cathy sisters, her experience has been marked by the harshness of her world, growing up poor and without parental support. In *Edith Jackson* Guy explores the last of the three elements of reconciliation—reconciliation-with-the-world. Making choices and assuming responsibility for self are Edith's particular challenges, but in the context of the trilogy, reconciliation-with-the-world subsumes awareness of self and relationships with others.

The novel continues the story of Edith Jackson's life begun in *The Friends.* Although structurally there are three distinct blocks of action in this work as there are three and two, respectively, in *The Friends* and *Ruby,* it seems significant that each of the three here is designated as a book rather than as a "part," as they are in the other novels. The terminology subtly reinforces the sense of the three novels as episodes in one larger story. There is an implication that all things will come together here as we follow Edith's life from early spring through year's end. In book 1, "Foster Family," Edith and her three sisters are in a foster home in Peekskill, New York; her baby sister, Ellen, has died of malnutrition and her brother, Randy, has been shot. By cajolery, threats, and bullying the social worker, Mrs. Brown, Edith has managed to keep her dwindling family together through several foster placements and months of waiting in the Institution. Edith optimistically believes their new home in Peekskill is an environment in which her sisters will have a chance to grow, but the unfolding events in the novel prove just the opposite.

Life in Peekskill disintegrates a little at a time. Edith's sister Minnie grows close to a white schoolmate. Bessie withdraws into fantasies and lies. Suzie simply builds her ego and existence on the life of her sister Minnie. Edith feels responsible for all of them, but also feels more and more shut out. When Bessie disappears with a friend of their foster mother's, life in Peekskill collapses. The girls are returned to the Institution where the family is finally split apart. Left alone and responsible only for herself for the first time, Edith faces the challenges and the perils of choice and self-responsibility.

The book dramatically exposes the culture, consequences, and institutions of poverty through the events in Edith's life. Proceeding more episodically than the earlier books, the novel packs less emotional power than either *Ruby* or *The Friends,* but from start to finish Edith's dilemma is vividly realized. She is the target of sexual harassment and inter- and intraracial prejudice. She confronts the very real problems—teen pregnancy and lack of education—that often plague young women in poverty situations, problems that lead almost inevitably to life as wards of the welfare system. As usual, Guy leaves the final resolution of Edith's dilemmas in the open realm of the reader's imagination.

Edith Jackson is the most extensive delineation of the orphan's experience that Guy has produced. Edith's enforced independence owing to her mother's death and her father's absence is an experience Guy knows well. In the novel these special circumstances heighten the protagonist's sense of family responsibility, shape her character, and create personal pitfalls as well. Edith is consumed by feelings of responsibility for her sisters, giving little thought to her own growth and adjustment. Her future seems unimportant compared to her mission: to take care of the children. Years of living a life that has seemed to offer her no other option but that of mother to her siblings has not only foreshortened her perspective on life but narrowed her sense of herself. For Edith there is only duty:

> Duty from the time I looked up and saw the world. Duty to cuddle, but never be cuddled. Duty to carry, and never be carried. To change diapers, to wash clothes, to clean, to teach. While that sick old man and sick woman sat around getting sick, sicker, old, older—then dying. (69)

Although Edith's family relationships and the tragedies and successes that befall her sisters are central to the book, this is ultimately a novel about Edith and her growth toward a life of choices and self-responsibility. As an objective commentator in the book, the black lawyer, Mrs. Bates, expresses its central vision: "It's a matter of choice. You cannot plan a life on raising your sisters simply because you have no choice. Nor can they think of living stuck to you because they had no choice." What she describes is an existential situation—choose, shape your life, or become one of the "faceless statistics." Love and responsibility are the great imperatives in Guy's works, and the reader is left with no doubt that they are the ultimate *good* consequences of individual choice, rather than burdens to which the individual is fated.

Guy's understanding of race, sex, and class and social institutions, life expectations, intraracial conflict, and the blight in the inner city is marshaled to present a realistic treatment of the theme of reconciliation with the world through individual choice. Imagery, irony, perspective, and juxtaposition of action all work together to support thematic development. Guy's use of perspective, for example, confers an important advantage. Edith is a strong-willed and colorful character and her first-person narrative is intense and personal. This point of view enhances the device of diminishing visibility—the loss of will or being expressed in figurative language—which is central to the revelation of theme. Time and the fate of the orphans conspire to pull the small family apart: sister Minnie chooses a white adoptive family; thirteen-year-old Bessie is found dead after disappearing with their foster mother's friend; and Suzy becomes a runaway when she is separated from Edith and placed with a new foster family. By the end of the novel, the Jackson family has literally vanished.

In her customary fashion Guy, through clues, introduces the reader to the skeleton of the conflict in the early pages of the novel. The order, content, and approach to character descriptions in the first chapters are illustrative. The narrative opens with Edith's whimsical description of a handsome, but reluctant, churchgoer; she has dubbed him "Mr. Brown." Edith does not know his identity and there is no indication of his potential significance in her life. Portraits of each of Edith's family members follow. Interestingly, the only common element in the descriptions is her insistent assertion that none of the family is interested in "dudes." In addition, each word portrait is concise, direct, and informative—except one. Only the final description—that of Edith—is different. Rather than a straightforward presentation of herself, she takes a more oblique approach, describing herself only through her description of her sister Suzy.

> Suzy looked more like me than the other two did. She was plain, brown-skinned, with short, nappy brown hair that even hair straighteners didn't manage. But Suzy had long legs, and I knew they would push her far higher than my five feet three inches by the time she reached my age, seventeen. . . . I guess Suzy's looking like me had made me want her to be smart on her own, do things I hadn't been able to, on account of having to look after all of them. (5)

Three characteristics are common to all the descriptions: the other-directedness, the maternal flavor, and the denial of sexual interests. In drawing her character, Guy makes clear the fragile self-image, low expectations, and veiled hopes that are the results of a life of poverty and prejudice. Edith's indirect self-description exemplifies her commitment to family first. She is never central; her needs are never important; her expectations are always tied to her responsibilities to others. Like Ruby, in the second novel, Edith defines herself and her expectations in terms of others. Edith's hopes for her sister Suzy, expressed in her description, reveal the depersonalizing results of this kind of life. Describing Suzy as "Minnie's Shadow"—her existence simply a reflection of sister Minnie—Edith seems to see Suzy as a younger version of herself, a child without a childhood, becoming a caretaker for others.

Edith's double-duty description of Suzy and herself has almost a maternal feeling. She is a surrogate mother for her sisters, and so bound to that commitment that she refuses to think of any other relationship or option; a career, love, marriage, possibly children of her own, do not fit in her life. But her laudatory description of the young man in church, Mr. Brown, as well as her constant assertions of disinterest in dudes, indicates the ambivalence of her feelings. The information and the manner of presentation, along with Guy's rendering of Edith's hard-bitten street language, combine to capture the essence of her character. In this first chapter three intersecting areas of conflict in Edith's life are suggested: self-image, sexuality, and choice. Two of the three—image and sexuality—are a continuation of central themes from the first two books in the trilogy.

Evidence of these three conflicts is apparent early in the family's experiences in Peekskill. The instability of their lives has made maintaining (or developing) a strong sense of self difficult, especially for the younger girls. The home, which they share with two other foster children, is their third placement in three years. Their status as foster children makes them fair game for abuse. Even the local minister, Reverend Jenkins, "rubs down" their pride while he seizes every opportunity to pursue Edith's substance (sexually harassing her) rather than her soul. Rejection erodes their self-confidence: Mother Gilmore is gone and Mother Pratt is gone, while months have been spent waiting for this new "home" with Mother Peters. Guy's ironic use of the title "Mother" for the various foster home hosts is made more ironic by what Edith describes as "the straightening fact" that "with one hundred eighty dollars a head per month, some folks were always willing to take [them] in, especially when she did the caring for [her] sisters and seeing that the work got done" (18). "Mothering" in these circumstances is reduced to a matter of dollars and cents, and even at the going rate the girls have been unable to keep a home.

The "rubbing-down effect," which has always been a part of their poverty-stricken existence, is even more evident in Peekskill, perhaps because of the contrast between the clean, green, safe suburb and their old home in Harlem. The results are inevitable. Bessie compensates with elaborate fantasies about her mother, fantasies that fail to dispel her doubts about her own self-image: "Edy, why you figger Mama had such good hair and ours turned out so nappy? . . . She had such pretty hair, she was so light-skinned—and we all come out brown with this bad hair" (29). Although Edith is surprised by the fantasy, she recognizes the source. Those with light skin and soft hair had always been envied and looked up to, while those such as herself were the butt of cruel jokes.

Even more insidious, from Edith's point of view, is the pulling apart of the family. Minnie, serious and studious, is increasingly interested in her new white friend, Judy. Bessie's changing behavior—the lies, the antagonism, the fantasies, and the fuzziness—reveal Edith's diminishing power over her sisters. She is hurt by Bessie's assertion: "You don't know me, see. You sure don't know me." She is sometimes ambivalent too, wanting to "break out, leave the house and family" but feeling compelled to find "a job to make it possible to take care of the kids instead of letting them be shifted around." The lawyer, Mrs. Bates, verbalizes Edith's concerns and doubts but also challenges her.

> They [your sisters] will grow, Edith, get big. But raising them?
> What guarantees that any family of four will march to the
> same rhythm? Particularly when the one doing the raising

hasn't developed a tune? . . . You have to know that there are other things you can do. . . . In this poverty situation, orphans—the abandoned ones—are by far the most vulnerable . . . meaning they can most easily be used; they melt more easily into that mass of numbers called statistics—faceless statistics. And nothing is worse than being one of the faceless. (52)

The device of diminishing visibility is used skillfully and naturally throughout the novel. The imagery—"rubbing down," "shadowed," "faceless," "invisible,"—is not forced. It is the antithesis of growth and development and naturally expressive of the results of the threats and dilemmas so vividly realized in the story: rejection based on color, class, race, or orphan status; sexual abuse, teen pregnancy, institutionalization, hopelessness. The overwhelming sense of disintegration reflected in the imagery is subtly and progressively reinforced through dialogue and action.

Edith remembers her father—an old man sitting with his back to his children—so overwhelmed by life that he had only the strength to do his duty, "no words, no kisses, just duty." One day he had simply disappeared. She feels her own lack of power and substance in the attitudes of the police when her sister, Bessie, disappears. The words "foster children" trigger a change in their attitude to "instant boredom;" the children are dismissed, all of them, "with a wave of [a] nightstick." Dematerialized in this way, the children feel a need to sit close, to touch bodies, "to prove [their] flesh was real like other folk." Their petty jealousies and occasional racial taunts are forgotten as the children feel their essential kinship. Edith confronts facelessness most devastatingly however, in Mother Peter's lack of response to Bessie's disappearance. Their foster mother's blind acceptance of Bessie's loss, caused by her willing use of the thirteen-year-old to hold on to her friend Uncle Daniels, indicates that she does not think of the girls as real people. With Mother Peter's fantasy life with Uncle Daniels gone, life in Peekskill for the now smaller Jackson family is over, and they are returned to the Institution.

Mrs. Bates and her family, on the other hand, offer Edith a different perspective on life. An orphan herself, Mrs. Bates stands in stark contrast to the other females Edith has encountered. She is clear-eyed, responsible, and in charge of her life. She loves her family but also loves herself; she is respected in the community and returns respect and service to the community. She is a mother, but not the mythic mother Edith has tried to be to her sisters. Mrs. Bates's daughter describes her as a "force," someone to be reckoned with. This is basically in harmony with Mrs. Bates's image of herself. With Edith this forceful woman shares a kind of older sister to younger sister communion, their shared experiences as orphans binding them. Her interest and understanding draw Edith even when she does not like what the older woman has to say; she "had not been sent for. [She] had come" (50). In her role as objective commentator, Mrs. Bates directly, and occasionally heavy-handedly, comments on the important social issues raised in the novel. In the summer, once again back in the Institution, Mrs. Bates's letters are Edith's only concrete anchors to the world outside.

Book 2 of the novel explores the Institution as a halfway house on the way to facelessness in the outside world. The name "Institution," devoid of any specificity, reflects the symbolic nature of this picture of the orphan's experience. Similarly, the names of characters like the social worker, "Mrs. Brown," and even Edith's pet name for the young man she becomes sexually involved with, "Mr. Brown," are names that reveal the characters as symbols rather than individuals—part of the life-style that erodes Edith's sense of self.

The rubbing-down effect is graphically revealed in Guy's description of the Institution. There are no individuals here—only categories of society's wards. There are foundlings, juvenile delinquents, and Edith's special loves, the Institution babies. No expectations are nurtured here; residents simply grow out of the shadow of the Institution into invisibility. Or if they're bright enough or lucky enough, they join the world of real people who make decisions about their own lives. Minnie's brightness sets her apart; she chooses life with a white adoptive family and escapes the Institution. Mary Allen and Pip Squeak, Edith's Institution babies, experience no such success. They are unloved and uncared for; simply talking and walking like other children are not part of their image or expectations. In her role as surrogate mother to these two, Edith provides the love and care, the urge to grow and change, that she herself has not received. She yearns for a love that will change her own life now that her sisters are gone and she alone remains.

Edith pushes her two Institution babies to meet the meager goals—monumental for them—of walking and talking. The goals are obviously symbolic: real people stand on their own two feet and speak for themselves. The atmosphere of intensity Guy builds into the scene of Edith's final visit with her young charges reiterates the symbolic nature of these two challenges. Deciding that she must leave them, she puts the children to the test. The scene is cast as a sort of ritual of preparation. The effect is dramatically created through language appropriately paced to set a mood of intense anticipation.

> "Now," I said, grimfaced, serious, . . . "you listen Pip Squeak. You gonna walk, you hear me?" He stared at my face, felt my beat, held tight to my fingers setting his mind to it. . . . something happened in that room: cries, screaming, yelling, everything stopped. The room shrank from silence. Legs came around. . . . I never looked up . . . all my attention on Pip Squeak. He kept his on me. (110)

The children's small victories—a few steps and two broken but jubilant words—are Edith's victories as well. The children have "learned to live," and Edith, propelled by her own personal longings, takes her first tentative steps into the outside world where the choices she makes are for herself.

Book 3 focuses on Edith's innocence and lack of experience in making choices. It is the pivotal section of the novel. Although life and the Institution have taught Edith a great deal about street survival, they have taught her nothing about personal goals and how to attain them. Guy brings us full circle with Edith living in Peekskill again. In her effort to escape being placed with the lecherous Reverend Jenkins, she has returned to the Bates household. Ironically, her actions bring her into confrontation with the sexuality she has long denied as she is drawn into the selfish embrace of "Mr. Brown," Mrs. Bates's nephew. The world of sexuality and romantic relationships is unexplored territory for Edith. She is an innocent girl who sees James ("Mr. Brown") as the fulfillment of all her fantasies. She is blissfully happy with their "secret relationship," but her bliss is short-lived. James leaves for Harlem and Edith finds that she is pregnant.

Returning to Harlem with fantasies of finding James and getting married, she discovers the depths of her inexperience and vulnerability. James has used and abused her, and Harlem, her old home, has changed. The old neighborhood is a wasteland and even her friends, Phylissia and Ruby, have moved. Although finding Phylissia and Ruby is not difficult, the reactions Edith receives from Ruby's friends, and even from strangers, almost breaks her spirit. Pregnant and alone, the shroud of invisibility seems to be descending upon her life. As she looks at the people she encounters, "they walked by like they walked through [her], not seeing [her.]." Although Phylissia and Ruby are happy to see her, Ruby's snobbish friends "hadn't seen [her], had wiped [her] out." Even gentle Ruby subtly declares Edith different by suggesting that Edith should have her baby and go on welfare, while Ruby's own decision is to have an abortion so that she can return to college.

The road from Harlem to Peekskill to Harlem, indeed her whole life, seems only to have prepared Edith to join the rest of her family as "faceless statistics": her father, "shuffling out of the door and never coming back, a statistic; Randy, shot by a cop, a statistic; Ellen dead, malnutrition, a statistic; Bessie dead, a statistic; Suzy, a missing person, a statistic." Only Minnie was different, "she had made a choice."

Minnie, although she has chosen a new family, becomes the link to keep the Jackson family in touch. The irony of Minnie, who has chosen adoption by a white family, assuming the role that might eventually help reunite the family is not lost on Edith. What Edith sees as family betrayal has spared Minnie the invisibility that the other family members experience, giving her a name and an address that can be traced. This kind of irony of intent versus actual effect supports the theme of choice and self-responsibility. Acknowledging her lack of preparation for motherhood or a self-supporting life, Edith decides to have an abortion and to reach out to her friend, Mrs. Bates, for help. Poised on the verge of invisibility—life as an unwed mother on welfare—she chooses rather to relinquish her place in the welfare line to another teenage mother. She is fully aware of the consequences of her choice and the years of work that lie ahead.

In *Edith Jackson,* the full scope of the problems affecting the years of growth for young women are explored not as isolated problems but, realistically, as intersecting issues. Each of the three novels in some way foreshadows conflicts and challenges yet to come. In the girls' reunion in *Edith Jackson* we are updated on the progress of their individual journeys. They have all come of age weaving the strands of their evolving selfhood into patterns of their own making. "Ruby [dreaming] from need" is still searching, seeking validation of herself in others, attending college to satisfy family and friends rather than herself. Phylissia, dream[ing] to be dreaming," confidently takes on the world as a place of adventure and excitement peopled with heroes and villains. Edith fighting her way out of the nightmare of poverty has taken a first step—her decision to have an abortion and to call Mrs. Bates for support—toward choosing and realizing her own dreams, her own self.

Conclusion

Guy's complex and credible black heroines have filled a void in the literature—a void Guy felt strongly as a young woman. Speaking out of her own awareness of this absence of black heroines, writer Alice Walker has praised Guy's work. In a review of *The Friends* she notes: "I relive those wretched, hungry-for-heroine years and am helped to verify the existence and previous condition of myself."[6] The existence and condition of young women growing up is the essence of the trilogy. Individually and as a unit the novels explore the process of reconciling self-images, relationships, and responsibilities (personal, familial, social) into a congruent, growing self.

Guy's special admiration for the black American woman is clearly evident in the characters—Daphne, Edith, Mrs. Bates—all strong distinctive individuals, but realistically portrayed with flaws as well as virtues. Guy has said, "I have always been the most profound admirer of the stamina, the grit of the black American woman. She is a strong individual, much different than her counterpart anywhere else in the world. She is someone of whom one need never be ashamed. She will always fill the place in any book—a history book, or fiction. The black American woman is the strength on which I believe the American society has survived."

Although Guy focuses in the trilogy on the experiences of young black women—their increasing need for independence and new relationships, peer pressure, growing sexuality, the conflicts of personal choice versus parental authority—the experiences are recognizably the same for all young people. Her sensitive and realistic handling of the special challenges of young women coming of age in the inner city mark her work as unique.

5. The Dis–Appearance

I think that at one particular point in my life I believed that
the individual had so much power to determine. But if they
cannot determine to love somebody else, and in some kind of
unity come together to meet a challenge—it's not true. I
would hate to write the story that would say that that thing
you call individuality is nothing but BS. I would hate to do
that! One fights against it. That you're just a little something—like a little ant, you find yourself here and you shuffle
around very busy until somebody puts a foot on you or something like that. And that's life! It makes no sense to me.

Rosa Guy

Rosa Guy knows the inner city. She knows Harlem, its sounds
and sights, and its people. Although she has been especially sensitive to the experiences of young women coming of age in the
inner city, she has not limited herself to the exploration of the
female experience. She knows young men as well, their street-
corner parlance, their posturing, pains, and pleasures. She knows
the city's Wades and its Malcolms, and all those in between.

Her character Imamu Jones effectively displays her knowledge.
He is perhaps her most perceptive purveyor of the mind and movements of his famed urban neighborhood, Harlem. But he is also
an astute observer of the world outside. A character imbued with
the memories, experiences, pains, and joys of Guy's life in Harlem,
her travels throughout the South, and her vision of courageous

young people struggling for change, Imamu is the central character in Guy's last two novels set in Harlem—*The Disappearance* and *New Guys around the Block.*

Introduced in *The Disappearance,* he is our guide through the evolving Harlem of the seventies, exposing a devastating transformation in both the spirit and the physical appearance of the community. The Harlem of *The Disappearance* and that of *New Guys around the Block* are not the same, but neither is Guy's dynamic character, Imamu Jones. These two novels capture both the literal "disappearance" of the old Harlem community and the figurative "dis–appearance" of her characters as she unmasks the motives and emotions hidden behind unlikely countenances.

The Disappearance

dis ap pear v. to cease to be visible, to pass from sight or from existence . . . dis ap pear ance n.[1]

Guy's fourth young adult novel in the Harlem series turns upon this word and its interpretation. Its apparently straightforward meaning changes on close examination of its two major components:

Dis: an adjective-forming prefix meaning not, un, the opposite of.

Appearance: n. 1. appearing. 2. an outward sign, outward looks.[2]

With this simple but ingenious dual emphasis, upon both passing from sight and not being true to outward appearance, Guy trains her sight on a cast of characters in Harlem and Brooklyn to bring human nature sharply into focus. The novel's plot seems simple on the surface: streetwise Harlem teenager Imamu Jones, released into the care of a suburban Brooklyn family, finds himself accused when the family's youngest child disappears. But in reality, the novel is more complex. Operating on several levels, it is part of the historical chronicling of Harlem that Guy began in *The Friends,* it is a fast-moving mystery, and it is a symbolic study of human nature.

When Imamu Jones moves from Harlem to Brooklyn, the problems he encounters in his new environment are not unexpected. He clashes with Peter Aimsley, his foster father, and he is treated as an interloper in the neighborhood. As he has been recently acquitted of murder and robbery, his arrival has set the entire household on edge. As a new male in the community, he is also the focus of the attentions of the Aimsley family's seductive friend Dorabelle and the carefully restrained interest of the Aimsley's elder daughter, Gail. His refuge from the frustrations of his new environment is periodic escape back to Harlem. He also finds himself drawn to the comfortable home of Dorabelle, whose overt sexuality he finds both frightening and appealing.

It is on Imamu's return from one of his first Harlem escapes that he discovers that the Aimsley's daughter Perk is missing, and he is suspected in her disappearance. Incredibly, his rescuer, Mrs. Aimsley, is his principal accuser. After a grueling interrogation/torture session with the police, he returns to Brooklyn intent upon finding the child. He is joined in his search by Gail, who has more than a sisterly interest in him and is his only defender. What he uncovers is a tangle of deceptions. Perfect marriages and friendships turn out not to be so perfect, and surface appearances mask feelings and actions that are just the opposite. Imamu has escaped from physical surroundings that sometimes breed violently warped individuals like his childhood friend, Iggy, only to discover distortions and dangers in the seeming safety of his new surroundings. It is only his intelligence, his unique way of seeing—nurtured on the streets—that can unravel the mystery. The fast-paced developments from the time of his arrival to his uncovering the truth are riveting. Finding the key to the puzzle of Perk's disappearance places Imamu in grave danger but ultimately leads to the discovery of a tragedy: the child has been accidentally killed by her godmother Dorabelle.

A comparison of Harlem and Brooklyn is central to the novel

and elucidates its major theme. The deterioration of the Harlem neighborhood is made unescapably evident through comparison with the clean, safe environment of the Aimsleys' suburban Brooklyn community, but the novel drives home the point that loneliness, fear, and insecurity are *human* frailties that recognize no address. The theme is a natural extension of Guy's vision of the human experience, a vision that declares love and responsibility to be the highest imperatives and that challenges us to acknowledge our common humanity.

The Disappearance echoes the theme Guy first explored in *Bird at My Window*—the impact of poverty and prejudice on youth in the ghettos—but it offers a more optimistic variation. The mystery that Guy unfolds in Brooklyn is given depth by the ironies revealed when the suburb and the ghetto are compared. Human motivations and emotions are similar, even though the conditions are not the same. The more refined and successful lives of the Brooklyn residents provide window dressing that masks motives. The discrepancy between appearance and reality prompts the reader to see the social masks we all wear in an entirely new light. Furthermore, indicative of the greater optimism of *The Disappearance,* Guy's streetwise protagonist, Imamu, is not portrayed as a deprived and destructive ghetto youth; rather, he is mature, intelligent, and proud. He has mined some advantages from his disadvantaged life.

Guy realizes her theme in *The Disappearance* by establishing a series of parallels between character, events, and situations in suburban Brooklyn and Harlem. A selective omniscient narrator controls the point of view. The usefulness and effectiveness of this kind of shifting perspective is clearly revealed in the two introductory chapters. As in her other works, Guy here effectively gives the reader the germ of the story: setting the scene, recapping the necessary background, and foreshadowing the conflicts to come. In these two parallel chapters the motivation for Imamu's departure from Harlem and hints of future conflicts are suggested.

Each of the two chapters focuses on the morning that Imamu is scheduled to report to the Aimsleys' home. Chapter 1 reveals the day from Imamu's perspective. Alone in the dark, dirty Harlem apartment he shares with his wino mother, he thinks of her. He recalls their past together—before her drinking—and his growing ambivalence toward her. The chapter closes on a note of conflict as his drunken mother and a wino companion arrive at the apartment. Strong emotions and the possibilities of violence are explosively introduced as Imamu's mother cuts short his threats to her wino friend with her taunt: "Gonna what? Gonna kill him too?" (8).

The contrasting chapter focuses our view of the immaculate Aimsley home in Brooklyn through the consciousness of their elder daughter, Gail. The family, which includes Gail, Mr. and Mrs. Aimsley, and their younger daughter, Perk, has gathered, along with their voluptuous friend Dorabelle. Only Mr. Elder, a family friend and roomer, is absent. As they tensely await Imamu's arrival, Gail's thoughts are also on her mother—her motivation for inviting Imamu, the small quirks of her behavior. In the final pages of the chapter strong emotions and a hint of violence are echoed in Brooklyn. Peter Aimsley's feelings about Imamu's impending arrival explode at his wife's euphemistic description of the boy's criminal record. Brutally exposing Imamu's acquittal for murder and robbery, he releases a mixture of tension and anger over the decision to bring Imamu home and expresses his fear of this youth from the streets. This is the tense situation into which Imamu walks.

Guy makes every word count in this tautly constructed novel. The imagery she uses in describing the Aimsleys' immaculate house is as sharp and clear as the plastic that covers the furniture in their home. With the exception of one unframed original painting, the room with its reproductions of "famous paintings gleam[ing] respectfully from shiny frames" is a model of restraint, civility, and cleanliness. Ann Aimsley is the master decorator in the house, and the results of her efforts best depict the designer herself. Only she, a "plain, intelligent" woman bending to pick up minute specks from the carpet, could live in this "well-kept, well-kept up" house with the "sense of conforming to the modern health standards." Here "an everyday sameness prevailed, cloaking the family in a sort of perfection" (15). Guy's word choice here is in stark contrast to her dark and dingy description of Imamu's Harlem: "The gray morning hulked outside the windows as though dreading to enter" this room where even the sheets on his bed had turned a dark gray. Loose plaster, exposed boards, and cockroaches complete the squalor.

Guy's imagery not only depicts the physical differences in the two households but is doubly effective in characterization. The characterizations so economically begun in her cataloging of the interior decor of each of the homes are enhanced by yet another view. Imamu, in his emotion-charged thoughts, compares this perfectionist wife, mother, and community worker to his own pathetically drunken mother. He has encountered no one quite like Ann Aimsley—except his mother *before* she began to drink. In her "smart suits with her silk blouses" (87) Mrs. Aimsley commands respect. She is caring, intelligent, and concerned; she is the mother of his fantasies. But he finds that her behavior is not dependable. She is sometimes indecisive, vague, and insensitive. Imamu marks the changes, even identifying her fuzziness and lack of knowledge with her everyday attire: "If she had on her other togs, she would have remembered . . . the name and the date. That kind of talk went with her housedresses" (98). Imamu's unrealistic view of Ann Aimsley offers insights into his own character as well.

Guy's style reflects her background and experiences, especially her island past. Apparent are an obvious love for language and an ability to re-create the sound and the sense of everyday speech. The reader can note in this novel, as in Guy's others, some consistent patterns in her use of imagery. The imagery of nature— trees, plant life, the sea—is clearly reflected. In *The Disappearance,* the natural environment is an antidote to the hardening effect of the streets. Imamu feels the difference in Brooklyn: "He started back towards the place he had come from, wanting to go back, wanting to walk up that quiet treelined street where the trees were planted so close they acted as a shelter. He liked the feel of being part of a full grown tree . . . it gave you strength— strength rising from the roots" (53). The use of lush, earthy island colors—red, yellow, orange, green, brown—in her descriptions are almost an index of pleasure. They resonate with memories of the island. (The Blue Basin described in a daydream in *Ruby* is one of Trinidad's most spectacular natural features.) Guy uses the island colors as symbols of pleasant environments and as identifying features of visually appealing people. Dorabelle dresses in a "shiny red housecoat" when she entertains Imamu in her home, which is decorated in oranges and browns, accented by red. The color motif even provides a significant clue in Imamu's solution of the mystery. He recalls Dorabelle's "dis-appearance," her uncharacteristic dress and look, on the day Perk was first missed. With "her head wrapped with a black cloth" and wearing "a gray, loose-fitting smock [which] hid her figure," Dorabelle that day had not "fit the picture he had of her." (75). Later he surmises that her head was wrapped to hide her baldness; Perk's discovery of that baldness led to the child's death. There is irony in this paradox of appearance acting as both cause and solution in the mystery of the missing child.

Of course, Guy is an astute observer of the ironies in life. She handily reveals them through careful dramatic sequencing and realistic dialogue employing West Indian and black American idioms laden with double meanings. She excels in the structuring and positioning of the innocent statement, situation, or action that later proves to be important. The surprising turn of events in an embarrassing and funny incident in Harlem involving Imamu and Gladys, an old friend, is a case in point.

While playfully flirting with Gladys, Imamu accidentally pulls off her fake ponytail—the source of her new look and an object of vanity. He is stunned by her angry reaction: "he looked up just in time to see her fist coming at him." This encounter ironically parallels and presages the bizarre encounter with Dorabelle that crystallizes Imamu's theory about Perk's disappearance. The irony of a concern over femininity and beauty evoking violence is apparent in both situations, although tragically so in the case of Perk and Dorabelle. Perk's death is brought on by vanity gone amok. When the child accidentally discovers her godmother's secret baldness, Dorabelle in a fury shakes Perk so hard the child falls and hits her head. Dorabelle's violent reaction is a replay of

Imamu's experience with Gladys. The location and the characters differ, but the motives are the same.

This kind of comparative situational irony is part of the novel's basic structure. As in life, emotions are compelling forces in the lives of Guy's characters. Aware that inner emotions are not always in tune with conscious behavior, owing to inhibiting social expectations and self-protectiveness, Guy capitalizes on the incongruities. Delving beneath the surface of characters and events, she exposes the unusual, the bizarre, the unnatural circumstance as it occurs in everyday life. "It is a question" she says, "of seeing the ugliness in myself, and understanding this ugliness in people. And seeing the facades that we've hidden behind. And it's intriguing to me. . . . So I'm always looking, looking behind the mask. Its an awful thing, but I see it easily."

Through her juxtaposition of the "normal" and what has been called by some critics the "grotesque," Guy makes strong statements about our common needs and humanity. Loneliness, fear, false pride, frustration, alienation, anger, and insecurity—all emotions as normal and natural as their more positive counterparts—can move individuals to acts and judgments that can have awful consequences, whether these individuals live in the ghetto or in the suburbs. Similarly, the social grotesqueries of poverty and race, class, and sex bias can thwart personal development and sabotage dreams, triggering powerful emotional responses. The emotional kinship between Gladys and Dorabelle, Anne Aimsley and Imamu's mother transcends class differences. Human frailties set off the events that lead to Mrs. Jones's escape into alcoholism. The same human frailties lead to Perk's tragic death in Brooklyn and revelations about the Aimsleys' secure life.

Guy builds dramatic tension to a climax in *The Disappearance* with meticulous care. Gradually unmasking her characters and revealing their fears and deceptions, she shows the mounting cost in human misery. The sick pride and festering insecurities of Dorabelle are exposed in both her response to Perk's discovery of her baldness and her irrational decision to bury the child after the accident occurs. Although the fall has been a tragic accident, Dorabelle's compulsion to keep her shameful secret unexposed overwhelms both logic and grief. Imamu's efforts to solve the mystery of the child's disappearance lead to additional revelations. The longstanding jealousy between Mrs. Aimsley and Dorabelle; the discovery of the years of silence in the household of the Aimsleys' neighbors, the Briggses; and the lifting of the cloak of secrecy surrounding the debilitating disease that has struck Dorabelle and Mr. Elder are all harbingers of the tragedy Imamu finally uncovers. Although the violence in the novel, when it comes, is real and raw, it is not sensational; the reader has been well prepared. The scene of Imamu's rescue from the half-crazed Dorabelle and the climactic discovery of the young child's grave is as cathartic as Dorabelle's shriek of agony. As Imamu says in the concluding chapter, "It just had to be, that's all."

Guy's refusal to shrink from the violent and the ugly in life and, consequently, in her books has not gone unnoticed by the critics. Reviewer Robert Unsworth questioned the "down" ending of *The Disappearance*.[3] Fritz, although impressed by its power, was not sure that readers younger than twelve would understand its message.[4] But the interpretation of the ending as downbeat is debatable. Moreover, these concerns do not take into consideration Guy's broad sense of her audience. Discounted is the multileveled structure of the novel. The book can easily and enjoyably be read as a suspenseful, realistic murder mystery by younger readers who may not understand a larger message. The deeper level is there, however, for readers who look for it.

The rich symbolism that forms the deeper level of the novel's meaning is often overlooked. Exploration of this symbolic level offers the rewards of continuous discovery. There is an integral relationship between character, situation, and action in the novel; its second level of meaning works because of these connections. Symbol in *The Disappearance* arises out of essential elements in the characters' lives. The one original painting in the Aimsley's house is a good example. It is intimately tied to characterization, setting, and situation. It immediately captures Imamu's interest on his arrival, piquing his curiosity. At a distance it seems only an artist's vision of huge, towering waves breaking upon the shore.

But subsequent examinations reveal that human figures are the substance of the waves—whether as victims or controlling forces, he cannot be sure. His developing understanding of the painting corresponds to the evolution of his understanding life in this deceptive Brooklyn neighborhood and, ultimately, of the mystery of the young girl's disappearance. Ann Aimsley's ownership of the painting, as her daughter Gail alone understands, is a result of her relationship with yet another young man from the street, a young man who, like Imamu, Ann Aimsley had befriended and then accused.

The painting itself mirrors the emotional intensity of the novel and reflects the commonalities of the human experience. The characters in the book, like the figures in the painting, are overwhelmed by loneliness, fear, pride—powerful forces that sometimes push them to commit terrible acts, whether they live in Harlem or Brooklyn. It is an intensity and an awareness that Guy felt strongly:"Writing the book, I had the feeling of it [the painting]. It was an overpowering feeling of being overcome by the surge of life that is cracking us all up as we laugh—unaware or aware. But we're all going into [it], being crushed by the same forces."

Imamu finds the meaning of the painting by resisting it, struggling against its seductive pull, the overpowering urge to give in to its surface meaning. It is only when he looks closer beyond the surface that its real meaning becomes clear. The painting is an artistic representation of life, of people confronting seemingly overwhelming forces and coping or not coping in their own ways.

Such symbolism is reflected in other aspects of the novel as well. The title, *The Disappearance,* certainly expresses the reality of this novel in which nothing is as it appears. What is apparently a painting of a raging surf is actually an artist's representation of the human experience. Ugliness, so artfully hidden in the Brooklyn neighborhood, is not readily apparent to the casual observer. Similarly, the contrast between the accidentally acquired piece of original art and the reproductions of famous paintings with which Ann Aimsley has decorated her spotless, plastic-covered living room enhances the portrait of a desperately insecure woman hiding behind her diligently maintained image of perfection.

Of course, Imamu, like the painting, is the lone original in a cast of characters who are all in disguise. He is the "ignorant" street boy but refutes the belief that street people are universally slow thinkers with simplistic interests and ideas. The street has given him some advantages, including a raw dialect with which Imamu dominates the novel. His insights focus our attention, often drawing us up sharply and making us pause to rethink a situation, or ponder an emotion. The dialogue is gritty, often coarse, but the sound and the meanings are vivid.

Imamu's intelligence extends beyond a simple understanding of the street to thoughts and perceptions about the world at large— about war and economics, the politics of the country and their impact upon him: "Seemed that folks set rules with evil intentions. Like fighting to keep young dudes from working and getting paid decent, then passing laws to keep old studs on the jobs" (157).

The gritty and unpolished rhetoric of the street-corner philosophers like his friend Al Stacy demonstrates a native understanding of the social forces that control their lives, belying their reputation as disadvantaged and unaware.

> "Keep the streets full of poor suckers—in their place. That keeps the jails running; troops at the reach of the army. Put poor dudes to work and screw the economy? All them policemens out a work? All them judges out a work? Them lawyers? And don't even start talking about them half-assed politicians. Baby, the life of the country depends on you being out of work!" (157)

Author Marge Piercy has described fiction as a way of inducting the reader into cities other people know,

> people who speak another language, people who construct the world on different forces and different necessities and different desires, people who live down streets you fear or streets who fear you . . . persuading people to cross borders of alienation

and mistrust into the existence of someone in whose mind and body they may find it enlightening to spend some time.[5]

The Disappearance quickly and easily engages the reader's interest and facilitates this kind of social exchange. Imamu Jones reshapes our vision of life as he juxtaposes two very different social worlds through his actions, his thoughts, his words, and his perceptions of others. By novel's end, the lines between good and bad, ugly and beautiful, advantaged and disadvantaged, seem not so clear-cut. The camouflage of social well-being in one of the worlds has been stripped away to reveal the motives, fears, and emotions that move people wherever they live.

Although the major portion of the action in *The Disappearance* takes place in Brooklyn, the Harlem scenes effectively continue the sensitive and realistic chronicling of the neighborhood which Guy began in the trilogy. The Harlem streets of graceful brownstones and apartment buildings she described in *The Friends* and *Ruby* are distant memories now. They have already begun to deteriorate by the time Guy returns us to Harlem in *Edith Jackson*. Edith, for example, notes the open doors and the "graffiti scrambled over the outside of the buildings." By the time of *The Disappearance,* the deterioration has spread, transforming Imamu's neighborhood from home into a place his mother seeks to escape from through alcohol and a place Imamu finds hard to miss from his vantage point in the clean, green Brooklyn neighborhood.

New Guys around the Block

In the sequel to *The Disappearance, New Guys around the Block,* Guy returns Imamu to Harlem. It has changed again—for the worse. The neighborhood is crumbling around him, beginning with his own apartment. The ghetto has gone from dilapidation to disaster. Partially abandoned buildings dominate the garbage-strewn streets—havens for the addicts, treacherous playgrounds for children. After experiencing life in the suburban neighborhood Imamu sees the devastation with new eyes. He himself has changed. Although he has surrendered the well-cared-for, tree-lined streets of Brooklyn, he has taken something of its environment with him. He is exploring other options in life: books, a job, and new relationships, especially one with Gail Aimsley, his foster sister and girlfriend.

Imamu is fearful that the depressed environment will hinder his mother's recovery. Hospitalized after she fell into an alcohol-induced coma, she is now on her way to recovery. Imamu has promised himself that he will help her, beginning with a major clean-up and brightening of the apartment. Money and help seem to be the only obstacles to completion of the project. Then money for paint is provided by his friend Al Stacy who remembers Mrs. Jones from the old days. Ferguson, Imamu's fat, jovial, and work-shy friend, incidentally provides the help. He is orienting Olivette and Pierre Larouche, two "new guys on the block," when Imamu recruits him to paint. The four of them make an unusual team, even a productive one, until Iggy returns. A friend from Imamu's youth, Iggy has just been released from prison after committing one, possibly two murders. His presence heightens the tensions that already grip the neighborhood because of the "Phantom Burglaries."

A series of successful robberies of elegant apartment buildings downtown have baffled the police. With no clues and no suspects they have concentrated their investigative efforts in Harlem; all young male residents, even the fat and clumsy Ferguson, are suspects. When Imamu, like his friends, is finally picked up and questioned, he knows that painting will have to take second place to tracking down the Phantom Burglar.

The "investigation" takes Imamu out of his home turf into downtown New York in search of clues. On his first trip, with his new friend Olivette along to assist, the boys are arrested and booked for suspicion in the burglary case. Officer Brown, Imamu's old nemesis from his Brooklyn experience, is the officer in charge of the case; his presence is an even more compelling reason for Imamu to solve the seemingly unsolvable mystery.

Imamu's growing friendship with Olivette pays off when Olivette's attractive mother—at her son's insistence—persuades Officer Brown to arrange for Imamu's bail. Out on the streets again, Imamu sifts through possible suspects among the Harlem regulars. He is genuinely surprised when clues began to lead to Iggy and, by association, to Olivette's younger brother, Pierre. The disappearance of Imamu's old friend Gladys and the discovery of her unconscious body only hours after Iggy has loudly threatened her reinforce suspicions of his involvement. When Iggy is killed in a surprise showdown with the police, everyone is convinced that the Phantom has been caught. Only Imamu is disturbed by incongruities between the crimes and Iggy's life-style. His investigative instincts and his knowledge of the streets lead him to uncover the identity of Gladys's attacker and the real burglar. His new friend, Olivette, has been the mastermind behind not only the Phanton Burglaries but also the death of Iggy and the attack on Gladys.

As usual, Guy sets the stage rapidly in the first two chapters, introducing the major players, setting up the parameters of the mystery, and foreshadowing the events to come. Imamu's friend Ferguson, an especially appealing minor character, lends humor to the narrative. He is effectively used to balance our view of the Harlem community. Ferguson, like Imamu, represents the survival of a socially and economically healthy element in the community and serves as the interface between the novel's major characters. Unlike Imamu or Iggy, he has not been involved with crime, gangs, or drugs. Weighing two hundred pounds, he indulges his favorite pastime of eating. He does not have to fend for himself nor does he, since his mother, a nurse, provides him with everything he needs, and his weight and humor serve informally to sanction his differences. But even Ferguson is afraid of Iggy, aware of his destructive bent, his inevitable fate.

> The brotherhood Imamu belonged to was made up of tough guys. . . . That got all busted up—all on account of Imamu's boy, Iggy. . . . That's one stud who would be guilty even if he was innocent. And they letting him out. I'll tell you one thing,

when he heads for his best buddy, Imamu boy—you got a lot
of painting to finish. (36)

The mystery in the story hinges on the two newcomers, Pierre
and Olivette Larouche. They are strangers to Harlem but not to
inner cities of which they have seen many. Although his language
and demeanor do not reflect this fact, the elder Larouche knows
the inner-city experience firsthand. One inner city is much like
another, he tells Imamu—"ugly, destructive—of people, of families" (39). Imamu's personal knowledge of the truth of this assertion and his perceptiveness about character are the keys to
resolving the mystery of the Phantom Burglaries.

Characterization is the novel's strong point. Guy's characters—
sometimes ugly—advance the story through perceptively ren-
dered actions and reactions, but they also illustrate the often
deforming effect of the blighted neighborhood. Characters like
the foul-mouthed Gladys and the amazingly, almost painfully,
stunted Iggy are not gratuitously included. They are creations of
the environment: a tender, needy young woman behind a tough,
brittle exterior; a lonely, emotionally crippled man whose only
mode of expression is violence. They act and react as their lives
have shaped them; they arouse strong emotions in each other and
in those around them. Struggling simply to survive, they are both
unwitting pawns—victims—of the Phantom Burglar's plan.

As in *The Disappearance,* Guy's characters and their predica-
ments move the story beyond surface considerations. The commentary on such issues as victims and victimizers and social
responsibility is well integrated into the plot, a natural extension
of setting, characterization, and action. Olivette, the ingenious
burglar, sees his scapegoating of the stunted Iggy as a veritable
community service. As for Gladys, her very presence sets him on
edge. Coarsely provocative as a rule, she turns even more crude
and raw-edged when she is threatened or rejected, her foul language offending the toughest sensibilities. It is this behavior, as
much as her attempts to blackmail Olivette with her knowledge
of his guilt in the burglaries, that triggers his violent attack on
her. In either case, he finds both Iggy and Gladys expendable.

They are victims of their environments victimizing others; they will be no loss. But in the guise of the all-knowing, refined newcomer enlightening his unenlightened friends, Olivette raises thought-provoking questions about social responsibility, human potential, and the pervasive problems of poverty.

Olivette's charm, brilliance, and pomposity seem, initially, almost irritatingly strange, but they prove character-perfect as the story of the burglar/con artist/villain—a genius gone bad—unfolds. Guy develops this duplicitous character through an artful combination of Olivette's own speech and action, the perceptions of others, and comparisons of Olivette, his brother, and Imamu. The perceptions of Mrs. Larouche and Gladys are particularly significant since they serve as Guy's customary objective commentators. Imamu's initial wariness of the two brothers is reinforced early in the novel by Gladys's gritty, but head-on assessment of Olivette: "He ain't here in this neighborhood with all these junkies and stuff, because he's so damn innocent. Don't matter if he got them sad eyes and sweet face," she says (52). His mother's resentful, often conflicting descriptions of the family's unorthodox past also confirm that things are not as they should be. The jarring contrast between the two brothers—one urbane and literate, the other a gentle-faced street talker—reinforces this sense of duplicity. More significant, however, the just-below-the-surface tension that marks Olivette's relationship with his mother, his brother, and even Imamu confirms that there is more to Olivette than meets the eye.

Guy makes Olivette's sociophilosophical discoursing, an important part of his character, do double duty as well-placed social commentary and an invaluable clue to the true nature of his character. Describing his family's nomadic existence, moving from one inner city to another, he says at one point:

> "Poverty, Imamu, can turn friend against friend, mother against children—children against parents. When that happens, children can talk loud, act bad—but whatever the reaction, they are alone. And when they're alone, inside—anything or everything, happens. I'll always remember Brother Joseph—a Jesuit. A friend of Mother's . . . Oh, a lovely man. He came to

me, after I had had an illness—in New Orleans. 'Poverty,' he
used to say, 'is a crime against man, caused by men. . . . but
if the modern world is to be saved . . . man must attempt to
find a new way.' " (67)

Olivette, although misguided and criminal, is certainly not simplistic. In this respect he reflects and is symbolic of Guy's thematic
intent: human nature is not black and white and the interrela-
tionships between people are even more complex.

Guy's imagery in describing Imamu's environment recalls the
device of diminishing visibility so effectively employed in *Edith
Jackson*. It also reflects the sense of people caught in the grip of
powerful but unseen forces. Her highly connotative language is
chosen for maximum emotional impact and implication. The descriptions of the mid-morning movements of people and conditions
on Imamu's street, as he sees them from his bedroom window,
are illustrative. The buildings are "crumbling," "bombed-out
shells," "caves." They "give up ghosts," not people; the "screaming
laughter" of children is loud—"so happy, so carefree, so unaware
that they [are] being conditioned in the squalor of their caves to
take over when this generation of ghosts passe[s] on" (41).

This diminishing, dehumanizing environment haunts Imamu's
dreams. In the novel's opening scene he awakens horrified by a
graphic dream of being caught in the midst of a surging, terrified
pack of rats. The reality of this dehumanization is even more
horrifying. He finds himself too terrified to leave the house after
watching the frenzied looting of an accident scene. Guy's powerful
visual images induce horror as she vividly describes the looting
of the unconscious accident victims by residents of Imamu's street—
the friends of his youth. They "swarm" over the cars "like giant
ants, pulling, tugging at everything moveable," "leaving the figures, doll-like, naked, askew on the streets," "running over them,
stripping them . . . like swarms of locusts—eating." Imamu is
horrified that the people and the neighborhood he has known have
come to this. Only at Olivette's insistence is he able to leave the
apartment, to walk the streets again. It is also Olivette who fits
the tragic incident into a larger context reflecting Guy's global
perspective:

"They call it dehumanization . . . but it's just a case of victims victimizing the victimizers, isn't it? . . . Who is innocent, Imamu? Everybody is profiting from the swarm of locusts—as you call them. After all, money circulates. Houses are bought, landlords get rich, campaigns are paid for. . . . They're [the looters] out in the streets, hooked and bleeding to death. Most of them the waste of our inner cities. . . . It's in the nature of things. Human waste affects us all." (127)

The conflict between Imamu's growing awareness of the possibilities in life and the limitations of his environment is a key issue in the novel. It echoes a theme that reaches to the roots of Guy's own personal experiences and the Garveyite teachings of her youth. The violence, poverty, and hopelessness of Imamu's surroundings raise very personal questions for him—questions that directly affect his day-to-day survival. But there are few answers.

But why hadn't they cleaned up the addicts on his block—even those who sat nodding on the steps of the precincts? Why hadn't they jailed the pushers, put the dealers out of business? Made the streets clean? Why didn't the police catch the burglar instead of riding Imamu Jones' back! And suddenly Imamu admitted to the presssure on him, every time he walked the streets, to keep from being picked up, while his mother lay in the hospital—with no one around but him to care. (59)

His friendship with Olivette seems to expand that special part of himself that had developed out of his relationship with Gail and the Aimsleys. Imamu can discuss questions about day-to-day living with Olivette, opening up in a way he has previously been able to do only with Gail. In their discussions and Imamu's inner thoughts we see his fears and needs, as well as the awareness and insight that has saved him from the fate of his friends.

Characteristically, *New Guys* does not offer a neatly packaged, happy ending. Imamu never reveals the identity of the true Phantom, and Officer Brown is content to believe that the case has been solved. Charges are dropped against Imamu and Olivette, but the victimized Iggy is not vindicated. He is, as Ferguson has predicted, destined to be "guilty even if he is innocent." Nor have the conditions that produce the inner city's Iggys changed. Olivette, the disturbed young genius, disappears, moving on, no doubt, to some other inner city. The clean-up of Imamu's apartment, however, is nearly completed, and Imamu has hopes that his mother will be able to come home soon. He has plans—a job and possibly a new home in Brooklyn—the beginnings of his effort to reach for a better life, the first steps toward growth and new possibilities.

New Guys is especially expressive of the real evolution of life in New York's inner city after the turmoil of the sixties, the magnitude of the community's destruction changing Guy's conception of the community that she has so often and affectionately written about. Writer Toni Morrison, citing Harlem as "the closest thing in American life as well as literature to a Black city," has ascribed the affection of black writers for Harlem to their love for "the village within it: the neighborhoods and the populations of these neighborhoods."[6] This feeling of a "village within" has all but disappeared in Guy's conception of Harlem in *New Guys*. For the most part, Imamu experiences only frustration there. The friends of his youth are dead, in jail, or dying on drugs. Even his mother has become a casualty, though she is attempting to struggle back. His thoughts of Gail, vacationing in the Caribbean, and the Aimsleys' apartment in Brooklyn provide the most consistent escape from the devastation he sees around him. Imamu's plans to look beyond Harlem as he plans his future subtly reflect a change in direction in Guy's work as well.

Though not marketed specifically for young adults, Guy's 1983 novel *A Measure of Time* best reflects the disappearing "village within" elements that Imamu's Harlem lacks. Its appealing main character, Doreen (based on Guy's step-mother), and the brilliant and historically rich evocation of an earlier vital and vibrant Harlem make for a solidly good reading experience. The novel also stands as a fitting counterpoint to the deteriorating and destructive Harlem reflected in *The Disappearance* and *New Guys*.

6. New Directions

All these years I have been wondering—and grumbling—
about the reasons I had chosen, and stuck to, so low-paying,
so rigidly disciplined, so devastatingly lonely a profes-
sion. . . . Looking forward from my first book, *Bird at My
Window*—which I dedicated to Malcolm X—to those still to be
published, the one constant I lay claim to is *caring*.

Rosa Guy, "All about Caring"

In this world growing ever smaller and more vulnerable to
the holocaust that might mean its end, it is of the utmost importance that young adults break with prejudice—that value
system which creates the socio-economic pressures that man-
gle the minds of minorities and create the dangers of world
annihilation. A more profound understanding, a broader vision of those with whom we must share space between shore
and sea can only make a coming together easier for the battle
in which we all must engage if the world as we know it is to
survive. This, I suggest is the theme of most of my novels for
young adults.

Rosa Guy in *Literature for Today's Young Adults*

One year after *The Disappearance*, Rosa Guy published another
novel that contrasted greatly with the works that preceded it,
Mirror of Her Own. It was the first of Guy's novels to be set
entirely outside of Harlem and her only work that did not feature
a black protagonist. Although the novel's focus on a young wom-

an's growth and the status of the outsider repeated the emphasis and interests of her earlier works, the treatment was substantially different. Guy's central vision was unchanged, but the publication of this book reflected the beginning of a move away from the inner-city setting that had shaped her life and her artistic development up to now.

Mirror of Her Own

Set in Oakbluff, an affluent community on Long Island, *Mirror of Her Own* focuses on seventeen-year-old Mary Abbott's attempts to grow outside the shadow of her beautiful and self-assured older sister, Roxanne. The opening scene in which the two face each other in a mirror as Roxanne applies her makeup symbolizes the story's central conflict. In this brief scene Guy introduces the protagonist, her sister, and the insular world in which they have grown up. The girls are discussing Roxanne's summer romance with John Drysdale, Oakbluff's most eligible bachelor and the object of Mary's secret romantic fantasies. Roxanne's single-mindedness about her career and her disregard for John amaze Mary but also reinforce her hopes that one day "a prince—perhaps even John Drysdale— . . . might take her away" (8).

With prompting from her friend Gloria, Mary determines to change her life, to become part of the Oakbluff social circle to which Roxanne belongs. Doors open easily for "Roxanne's sister" and Gloria is invited along. Mary is neither comfortable nor confident with this posh crowd, however. On her first outing, which Roxanne has not been able to attend, Gloria's racist behavior is an embarrassment and Mary's overattentiveness to John Drysdale under the influence of wine and marijuana starts rumors.

Simultaneously changes take place at home. Roxanne is accepted for a fashion school in Paris, and the girls' normally placid parents are openly upset. Their attempts to dissuade Roxanne lead to revelations about Abbott family dynamics and the parents' secret plans for Roxanne's future. They are hopeful that Roxanne will marry John Drysdale so that she can restore the Abbott family's social position and secure the return of Abbott land illegally annexed by the Drysdales years ago. Realization of her own insignificance in her family's life is very painful for Mary, but the thought of her acceptance by Roxanne's friends comforts her.

Unaccustomed to her newfound social acceptability which rumors of her behavior with John have created, Mary revels in her place in the spotlight. One evening, under the influence of drugs provided by John, she loses her stutter and becomes the life of the party until she causes a small scene. A stunned and angry Roxanne turns on John and takes Mary home. Later that same night, still high from drugs, Mary escapes through her bedroom window and once again encounters John. He takes advantage of her condition to seduce her and then cruelly insults her the next morning by openly pursuing Roxanne, just hours after he and Mary have made love. Humiliated by John's brutal treatment of her, Mary runs away and becomes lost in the woods near her house, where she has a near-fatal accident. Yet she survives the physical and emotional injuries of this experience, emerging— we are asked to believe—with a clearer understanding of herself. Apparently, Mary now realizes that she has been living in her sister's shadow and denying her own worth as a person.

Mirror of Her Own is the least successful of Guy's books, falling short in areas in which she usually excels. The novel's most telling flaw is its weak characterization. The insecure Mary is the most fully drawn of the characters, but even she seems incomplete. She is plain, she stutters, she is easily bullied. Even in her private moments, with her writing, she seems uncomfortable and lacks self-confidence. In the opening scene when beautiful Roxanne leaves the mirror, "it seemed to Mary that a light had gone out. She turned to go to her own room, erasing her image from the mirror—a girl, stringy brown hair lank on her sloping shoulders, wearing faded jeans and a T-shirt stretched down over a flat chest." Mary is drawn as a passionless reverse image of Roxanne, but her weakness is her only character trait. We never see another dimension to her personality; we never understand what motivates her.

The Oakbluff social clique to which Mary would like to belong is an enigma, but her desire to join it is even more of a puzzle. The group is composed of visiting foreigners, such as the African Anikwi, and Oakbluff "residents" like Ron Holstein and John Drysdale who are rarely in town. The fringe members of the clique like Diane Cobb and Michael Stevens who are full-time Oakbluff residents have openly revealed themselves as racists and status-climbers; they routinely snub Mary until Roxanne begins to date John Drysdale. In reality, then, Oakbluff society has nothing to offer Mary. She is too timid and self-conscious to try her hand at tennis or join her sister on one of the group's trips to New York City. Their far-flung discussions of the role of Third World countries, as incongruous as they are, are certainly over her head. She is embarrassed to be seen with the summer's only royal guest, Anikwi, the African prince. She has avoided any interaction with the two black Americans who are occasionally part of the Oakbluff social scene, except to let her friend Gloria bait them. John Drysdale, who is a snob and a user of drugs as well as people, is the group's only attraction for Mary—an attraction that leads to humiliation and a close scrape with death.

Because Mary lacks the one ingredient that has marked all of Guy's previous characters—passion—she is manipulated and controlled by everyone. She herself cares about nothing. Told from Mary's perspective, the story is an endless litany of her woes and unfulfilled desires, about which she refuses to do anything. She does not even act upon her crush on John except when she is under the influence of drugs. Mary's response to the discovery of her parents' grand plan for Roxanne's marriage to John typifies her apathetic nature. Rather than openly express her anger and jealousy, rather than even question her parents' right to manipulate lives, Mary quietly nurses her hurt that she was not the one chosen as the future Mrs. Drysdale. Her extraordinary flatness and passivity make her totally unappealing.

Part of the strength of Guy's character development in the preponderance of her work lies in her ability to create realistic dialogue. She has said: "I love going into people's minds and snatching things from them. When I'm writing, I really go into my character. I just feel that this is the way they're going to say it, that's the way they *have* to say it." But her customarily flawless rendering of realistic dialogue enriched by well-integrated social commentary is absent here. Although there is a good deal of social and political commentary, it is spouted abruptly and unconvincingly at unnatural moments by unlikely people. A recovering Mary, for example, apologizing for not appreciating Roxanne's ability to recognize and survive the family's favoritism, is comforted with sisterly words interlaced with political and social commentary that is jarring in such an intimate context:

> Not just in this family, Mary—any family. Ring any doorbell. Knock on any door and you will find eyes looking out through layers of blindness. People refusing to see that the wealth, the power they worship has created the poor, the unfortunate which they hate. They never see the relationship between the two. (179)

Similarly, Roxanne's description of her father during a late night conversation about marriage and the future seems counter to both the mood and the emotions of the situation.

> I don't want to displease Dad. . . . But I don't know if I care— one way or the other. I used to—very much. But more and more I'm realizing I'm the daughter of the enemy. . . . So smug. Has ability but never tries. Has influence but refuses to use it—for change. He is the enemy of the people, Mary. (46)

The use of symbolism in *Mirror* is as problematic as the characterization. The symbols seem empty and without force when compared to the integral symbolism of Guy's earlier works. This is largely a result of a less coherent structuring of the novel. The details of the work do not fit together; there is no consistent level of actual meaning from which symbolic meaning can arise. The second chapter of *Mirror* offers a useful example: "James Abbott, a tall gaunt man, had long, sensitive fingers, clumsy in their shyness. They reminded Mary of her mother, of herself. His hands represented the Abbott family—except for Roxanne" (10). Here the symbolic nature of Mr. Abbott's hands is clearly stated. Much later in the novel Mary comments on them again, describing them, and presumably her family, as "weak and clumsy." Although sensitive and clumsy and weak are how we are expected to see this family, in actuality the unfolding action and Guy's characterization of the other family members are not in concert with this image. Adele and James Abbott are certainly neither sensitive nor weak. They handily, and without sensitivity, ignore the feelings of their children in their efforts to restore the lost Abbott image. Their efforts have been well planned and executed and they have effectively manipulated their children for many years. Thus, the description of James Abbott's hands, in failing to reflect his actual nature, is empty symbolism.

The symbolism of the mirror, reflected in the title, although more successful, points up a flaw in Guy's characterization that limits successful expression of the novel's theme. Roxanne Abbott is stereotypically perfect. She is too poised, too sure, too beautiful, and too assertive to be true. We are given no real basis for the development of her character, even if it were plausible. Given the manipulative, tradition-bound behavior of her parents and the sterility of the Oakbluff community, such perfection seems improbable. Roxanne is the symbol of perfection; a reverse, or mirror image, of Roxanne is a person with no personality, no spirit, no interests, and no confidence—Mary. Although the image of the mirror accurately symbolizes Mary's living in Roxanne's reflection, the level of actual meaning is unconvincing. One girl is too perfect to be believed and the other is so passionless that the reader cannot care about her fate.

The theme of Mary's self-discovery—her growth out of her sister's shadow—so important in Guy's other works, is never really developed in the novel. We are told only that succumbing to drugs Mary stumbles into a sexual encounter with John, is hurt and humiliated afterward, becomes lost in the woods, and, miraculously, emerges wiser. Neither are the various secondary themes of family relationships, choices, race/class prejudice and images effectively handled. Instead, weak symbolism and far too much undigested social commentary are used as short cuts with little or no support from characterization. The balance and integration that are so evident in Guy's earlier books are missing here, and the novel suffers.

Having moved, for the first time, outside her customary inner-city setting, Guy is able realistically to pinpoint the problems of an outsider in an affluent environment—family and social problems that are not unlike those experienced by some of her inner-city protagonists. However, she is unable to make her characters convincing and vital so that the reader believes in and empathizes with them. This failure of characterization is probably related to Guy's failure to keep within her creative range. As Robert Liddell has described it in his *Treatise on the Novel,* range is distinctly different from experience and is "probably a matter over which [a novelist] possesses little control." One's range as a novelist, that part of experience that one is able to use creatively, has generally been dictated by one's nature or early environment, and few forces, other than grief, can extend it.[1] The affluent setting of *Mirror* may not be beyond the scope of Guy's experience, but the flaws of the novel indicate that it may be beyond the scope of her creative range.

My Love, My Love; or, The Peasant Girl

Guy is more successful in her allegorical novel set in the Caribbean. Realizing her goal of sharing another side of herself, another facet of her multifaceted vision, she created *My Love, My Love; or, The Peasant Girl.* Meshing the many strands of her West Indian heritage—the oral tradition, the calypso, superstitions, voodoo, Catholicism, the luxuriantly vital, sometimes violent, natural environment—and her experiences as an orphan in a strange and unfriendly city, the novel is ostensibly the story of a poor but beautiful orphan who gives her life for love. In actuality it is an allegory on race and class bias and the need for love, understanding, hope, and patience in the world.

This tender but tragic love story, based on Hans Christian Andersen's "The Little Mermaid" is set on a Caribbean island called "the jewel of the Antilles." Desiree Dieu-Donne, a beautiful black peasant girl, orphaned when her parents are killed in one of the violent rain storms that often batter her island home, falls in love with a handsome Creole boy whose car crashes just outside her village. She nurses him back to health and pledges her soul to her patron god in order that his life might be spared from Papa Ge, the demon of death. She is heartbroken when he is taken back to the big city where he lives with his father, Gabriel Beaux-homme, a wealthy Creole landowner.

Against the best advice of her foster mother and the village elders, and after a fearful consultation with the gods, Desiree leaves for the city. She is convinced that the young Beauxhomme's life is in danger and only she can save him. Her journey includes the three classic encounters of fairy-tale journeys in which her beauty, honesty, and innocence win her advice, sustenance, or talismans to aid her in her quest. By one old woman, she is cautioned to have patience, by another, she is advised to couple patience with a wish, and from a third, she receives a special comb that accentuates her natural beauty.

In the city she must maneuver her way past brutal guards to get inside the gates that separate the Beauxhomme residence from the vendors and the poor. The red comb ensures her success. Once inside, she waits patiently for an opportunity to speak to her young man, living off the fruits from the grounds of the estate and sleeping in a crevice beneath his window. Although he does not recognize her immediately, he is taken by her beauty and the healing power of her gentle ministrations. Against the will of his father and his nurse, Desiree becomes his constant companion and eventually, to everyone's horror, his mistress.

Well fed and happy now, Desiree abandons her special comb, her last link to her old life, and patiently waits for the day she will become the true mistress of the great house. With the return of the young man's health, however, his father steps up his efforts to end his son's relationship with the peasant girl. When the young man's betrothal to the daughter of another wealthy family is announced, Desiree is removed from his side and housed in a small room down the hall. Growing unkempt and weak from despair, she is finally tossed outside the household gates by the brutal gatekeeper who has resented her presence among the well-to-do. Nursing a hope that the young man will yet proclaim his love for her, she dies on the day of his wedding, trampled underfoot by the peasants fleeing from the gate as mounted policemen clear the way for the wedding party.

In just over a hundred pages Guy powerfully expresses each of the central themes that have marked her previous works within the format of a tender and tragic love story. The story contrasts the life-styles of the haves and the have-nots, demonstrates the hardships of an orphan's struggle to succeed, portrays love ill-returned, and mourns the waste of goodness, youth, beauty, and love by the evils of poverty, greed, and prejudice. Guy's rich and lyrical language captures the natural beauty of the island, the intricate spiritual mix of voodoo and Catholicism, and the self-renewing spirit of life in harmony with nature.

Symbolism suffuses the story; names and dialogue, in the rich West Indian idiom, add new dimensions to surface events. The old storyteller, Monsieur Bienconnu ("knows well") has "lived long enough to see time chase time over and over again—and lived only to tell about it." Desiree Dieu Donne (which translates as "God-given desire"), although cast, on the surface, as a young woman tragically given over to a doomed love affair, symbolizes more. Madame Mathilde, the nurse, describes her as "the best of us":

> Desiree Dieu-Donne, you are the best of us: woven from the fragments of orphans; imbued with the swollen hopes, the courage of dreamers; sensitized with the hearts of lovers; made compassionate through the tears of the poor, mourning those lives wasted for having lived. All have washed over you, deceiving you into believing that all things are possible. You are the best in us—our humanity. (99)

Although in the tense battle between the rich and the poor symbolized by Desiree's experiences in the city, the rich seem in the end victorious, the very resilience of life commands the story. When Desiree dies, a swarm of butterflies appears, dispersing the

crowd and "flutter[ing] thickly over the body of the peasant girl."
Then a "promised storm [breaks] with a vengeance," seeming to
mourn her loss as "two drops of rain, resemb[ling] tears" fall on
her closed eyelids. The rain itself is symbolic, part of the promise
of life that Old Mama Euralie often expressed: "What storm is it
that doesn't in some way favor us peasants?" From its wind and
waters come materials for rebuilding—"fallen trees with which
to build, and leaves for roofs, and tools to rescue from the mud,
and of course the mud itself. Every day is followed by night, and
every night by day" (30).

This brief tale epitomizes the broad-ranging appeal of Guy's
work. It is not exclusively an adult, young adult, or juvenile novel.
Although the protagonist is sixteen, the style and themes defy
the application of age boundaries. Young adults accustomed to
novels that reflect their contemporary milieu may tend to over-
look this small gem, but those who sample it will be captured by
the tragedy, romance, and haunting message of the tale. Mining
her rich store of childhood memories, Guy has created a tale that
combines the mythology, experiences, and sensibilities of her Caribbean heritage with issues of contemporary relevance.

7. Conclusion

Rosa Guy's varied readership may be the most accurate measure of her success as a writer. She has made Harlem real for readers from Brighton, Massachusetts, to Brighton, England. Readership for her novel *The Friends* ranges from avid sixth and seventh-graders to appreciative adults. *The Disappearance* was selected as a best book by the Young Adult Services Division of the American Library Association, and two volumes of her trilogy have been on the syllabus of the public schools in Britain since the late 1970s. Her novels are included in bibliographies of black women's literature as well as feminist studies courses.

Her unique vision re-creates the complexities of the lives of young people growing up in the inner city within the context of the struggle to satisfy universally basic human needs and aspirations. The complex social terrain of the ghetto, to which she introduces many readers, reveals common challenges and choices. The popularity of Guy's work in so many communities and countries is a measure of the universal emotional truths she explores through the unique experiences of black and West Indian–American youths.

There is a compelling sense of continuity in her work. The rhythms and rhetorics of her island and inner-city pasts are woven throughout her writing. Her deeply felt concern for the loss of young talent and potential to the destructiveness of inner-city poverty, prejudice, and decay runs throughout her books. With sensitivity and compassion she portrays the experiences of young urban outsiders. Simultaneously, she chronicles the physical and emotional evolution—or disintegration—of the Harlem community.

The contrast between the natural, vital environment of the Caribbean islands and the cold, impersonal city life is evident in all her work. In her first novel, *Bird at My Window*, the contrast is cast in terms of nostalgia for the South: "You ain't never known the things we know. What it's like to live in a place where life is pretty . . . where there is a lot of green grass to play in and woods." In her trilogy and *The Disappearance*, the protagonists find comfort in memories of the island or respite in Harlem's parks. In *New Guys around the Block*, however, this connection to nature is absent altogether. The vital Harlem community that was such a large part of her life and the evolution of her work has finally disappeared completely. (She has recently finished a sequel to this book, *And I Heard a Bird Sing*, which completes her second trilogy.) In *My Love, My Love*, Guy shares another part of herself, returning to her roots in the West Indies.

The driving force that has kept Guy working is evident in her excitement about ideas for future books. "Writing has become my life," she says. Her rich background and varied experiences give her wide terrain to explore. She continues to write out of a deep sense of compassion and caring about people—especially young people—and a belief that writing should give the young "the broadest kind of understanding." This belief and the work that it has inspired has greatly enriched the literary options of young readers.

Notes and References

Preface

1. E.M. Forster, *Aspects of the Novel* (New York: Harcourt, 1927), p. 63.

Chapter 1

1. Thomas Page, *Selected Black American Authors* (Boston, 1977), p. 107.
2. Anne Commire, ed., *Something about the Author* (Detroit, 1976), p. 77.
3. Tony Martin, *Literary Garveyism* (Dover, Mass., 1983), p. 19.
4. Langston Hughes, "The Negro Artist and the Racial Mountain," *Nation* 122 (June 1921): 692–94.
5. Judith Wilson, "Face to Face—Rosa Guy: Writing with Bold Vision," *Essence*, October 1979, p. 14.
6. Maya Angelou, *Heart of a Woman* (New York, 1982), p. 85.
7. Commire, *Something about the Author*, p. 77.
8. *Ebony Pictorial History of Black America*, Chicago: Johnson Publishing, 1971, 2:200.
9. Ibid.
10. Ibid.
11. Rosa Guy, "All about Caring," *Top of the News* 39, no. 2 (Winter 1983): 94; hereafter cited in text as "Caring."
12. Wilson, "Face to Face," p. 14.

Chapter 2

1. Angelou, *Heart of a Woman*, p. 95.
2. Ibid., p. 103.
3. Ibid., p. 45.

4. Imamu Baraka, "Black Literature and the Afro-American Nation: The Urban Voice," in *Literature and the Urban Experience*, ed. Michael Jaye and Ann Watts (New Brunswick, N.J., 1981), pp. 153–54.

5. Brooks Johnson, "Books Noted," *Negro Digest*, 1 March 1966, p. 33.

6. David Llorens, "Seeking a New Image: Writers Converge at Fisk University," *Negro Digest*, June 1966, p. 62.

7. Guy, *Children of Longing*, p. xiii.

8. Wilson, "Face to Face," p. 14.

Chapter 3

1. Guy, "I Am a Storyteller," *Hornbook*, March-April 1985, p. 221.

2. Geta LeSeur, "One Mother, Two Daughters: The Afro-American and the Afro-Caribbean Female Bildungsroman," *Black Scholar* 17, no. 2 (March-April 1986): 26.

3. Rosa Guy, audiotape of speech for panel discussion of "Children's Writing Today for Tomorrow's Adults," *Boston Globe* Book Festival, 4 November 1984.

Chapter 4

1. Mary Helen Washington, ed., *Midnight Birds: Stories of Contemporary Black Women Writers*. New York, 1980, pp. xv–xvii.

2. Regina Williams, "Book Review: *Ruby,*" *Interracial Books for Children Bulletin* 8, no. 2 (1977): 14–15.

3. Ruby Dee, *"Ruby:* Notes on a New Novel," *Freedomways*, no. 2 (1976): 119.

4. Judith Mitchell, "Loving Girls," *Alan Review* 10, no. 1 (Fall 1982): 32.

5. "Review: *Ruby,*" *Publishers Weekly* 209, no. 16 (19 April 1976): 80.

6. Alice Walker, *The Friends*, *New York Times Book Review*, 4 November 1973, 26.

Chapter 5

1. *Oxford American Dictionary*, 1980, s.v.

2. *New World Dictionary*, 2d college ed. 1974, s.v.

3. Robert Unsworth, "Book Review: *The Disappearance,*" *School Library Journal,* November 1979, p. 88.

4. Jean Fritz, "Book Review: *The Disappearance,*" *New York Times Book Review,* 2 December 1979, p. 40.

5. Marge Piercy, "The City as Battleground: The Novelist as Combatant," in *Literature and the Urban Experience,* p. 210.

6. Toni Morrison, "City Limits, Village Values," in *Literature and the Urban Experience,* p. 37.

Chapter 6

1. Robert Liddell, *Treatise on the Novel* (London, 1965), p. 43.

Selected Bibliography

Primary Sources

1. Novels

Bird at My Window. Philadelphia: Lippincott, 1966.
The Disappearance. New York: Delacorte, 1979.
Edith Jackson. New York: Viking, 1978.
The Friends. New York: Holt, Rinehart, 1973.
Mirror of Her Own. New York: Delacorte, 1981.
My Love, My Love; or, The Peasant Girl. New York: Holt, Rinehart, 1985.
New Guys around the Block. New York: Delacorte, 1983.
Ruby. New York: Viking, 1976.

2. Anthologies, Essays

"Black Perspective: On Harlem's State of Mind." *New York Times Magazine,* 16 April 1972.
Children of Longing. New York: Holt, Rinehart, 1970.

3. Short Stories

"Wade." In *Ten Times Black.* Edited by Julian Mayfield. New York: Bantam, 1972.

4. Plays

Venetian Blinds. Produced in New York, Topical Theatre, 1954.

5. Speeches

"All about Caring." Speech given at the Young Adult Services Division Preconference on Booktalking, American Library Association, Philadelphia, Pa., July 1982. Published in *Top of the News* 39, no. 2 (Winter 1983).
"I Am a Storyteller." Speech given at Young Adult Literature Panel, *Boston Globe* Book Fair, 4 November 1984, Boston, Mass. Published in *Hornbook*, March-April 1985.

6. Unpublished Interviews

Norris, Jerrie. Audiorecording: Interview in Boston, Mass., 4 November 1984.
————. Audiorecording: Rosa Guy responds to follow-up interview questions, New York City, June-July 1985.

Secondary Sources

Books

Angelou, Maya. *Heart of a Woman*. New York: Random House, 1982.
Bone, Robert. *The Negro Novel in America*. New Haven: Yale University Press, 1965.
Commire, Anne, ed. *Something about the Author*. Vol. 14. Detroit: Gale, 1976.
Contemporary Authors. Vol. 17. Detroit: Gale, 1976.
Contemporary Literary Criticism. Vol. 26. Detroit: Gale, 1983.
Kirkpatrick, D. L. *Twentieth Century Children's Writers*, 2d ed. New York: St. Martin's, 1983.
Page, James. *Selected Black American Authors: An Illustrated Bio-bibliography*. Boston: G. K. Hall, 1977.
Wilson, Judith. "Face to Face—Rosa Guy: Writing with Bold Vision." *Essence*, October 1979.

Selected Reviews

Bird at My Window
Johnson, Brooks. "Books Noted: *Bird at My Window*." *Negro Digest*, 1 March 1966.

Redding, Saunders. "BookCorner: *Bird at My Window.*" *Crisis*, April 1966.

The Disappearance
Fritz, Jean. "Book Review: *The Disappearance.*" *New York Times Book Review*, 2 December 1979.
Heins, Ethel. "Book Review: *The Disappearance.*" *Hornbook*, February 1980.
Norris, Jerrie. "Urban Strife on Suburban Streets." *Christian Science Monitor*, 15 October 1979.
Unsworth, Robert. "Book Review: *The Disappearance.*" *School Library Journal*, November 1979.

Edith Jackson
Banfield, Beryle. "Book Review: *Edith Jackson.*" *Interracial Books for Children Bulletin* 9, no. 6 (1978).
Heins, Paul. "Book Review: *Edith Jackson.*" *Hornbook*, October 1978.
Lanes, Selma. "Book Review: *Edith Jackson.*" *New York Times Book Review* 2 July 1978.
————. "Main Events: Review, *Edith Jackson.*" *Essence*, May 1982.
Pollock, Pamela. "Book Review: *Edith Jackson.*" *School Library Journal*, April 1978.
Sutherland, Zena. "Book Review: *Edith Jackson.*" *Chicago Bulletin of the Center for Children's Books*, 32, no. 7 (March 1979).

The Friends
Heins, Ethel. "Book Review: *The Friends.*" *Hornbook*, April 1974.
————. "Lives against the Odds." *Times Literary Supplement* (London), 20 September 1974.
Walker, Alice. "Book Review: *The Friends.*" *New York Times Book Review*, 4 November 1973.

Mirror of Her Own
Shapiro, Lillian. "Book Review: *Mirror of Her Own.*" *School Library Journal*, May 1981.

My Love, My Love; or, The Peasant Girl
Blondell, Janet. "Book Review: *My Love, My Love.*" *Library Journal*, 15 October 1985.
Gropman, Jackie. "Book Review: *My Love, My Love.*" *School Library Journal*, January 1986.

New Guys around the Block

Flowers, K. "Book Review: *New Guys around the Block.*" *Horn Book*, June 1983.

General Background

Abramson, Doris E. *Negro Playwrights in the American Theatre: 1925–1959.* New York: Columbia University Press, 1967.

Ebony Pictorial History of Black America. Vols. 1–3. Chicago: Johnson Publishing, 1971.

Gayle, Addison, Jr. *The Way of the New World: Black Novels in America.* Garden City, N.Y.: Doubleday, 1975.

Halliburton, Warren. *Harlem: A History of Broken Dreams.* Garden City, N.Y.: Doubleday, 1974.

Hughes, Langston. "The Negro Artist and the Racial Mountain." *Nation* 122 (June 1921).

Jaye, Michael, and Ann Watts, eds. *Literature and the Urban Experience.* New Brunswick, N.J.: Rutgers University Press, 1981.

LeSeur, Geta. "One Mother, Two Daughters: The Afro-American and the Afro-Caribbean Female Bildungsroman." *Black Scholar* 17, no. 2 (March-April 1986).

Liddell, Robert. *Treatise on the Novel.* London: Jonathan Copley, 1965.

Martin, Tony. *Literary Garveyism.* Dover, Mass.: Majority Press, 1983.

Nilsen, Alleen Pace, and Kenneth Donelson. *Literature for Today's Young Adults.* 2d ed. Glenview, Ill.: Scott Foresman, 1985.

Quita, Craig. *Black Drama of the Federal Theatre Era: Beyond the Formal Horizons.* Amherst: University of Massachusetts Press, 1980.

Tate, Claudia, ed. *Black Women Writers at Work.* New York: Continuum Publishers, 1983.

Wade-Gayles, Gloria. *No Crystal Stair: Visions of Race and Sex in Black Women's Fiction.* New York: Pilgrim Press, 1984.

Washington, Mary Helen, ed. *Midnight Birds: Stories of Contemporary Black Women Writers.* New York: Anchor Books, 1980.

Index

About the Author

Jerrie Norris has been a children's librarian and librarian in public libraries in Boston and Cambridge, Massachusetts, and Atlanta. She has edited a book review column for the *Advocate,* the journal of the Southeastern Advocates of Literature for Children, and has written reviews for the *Christian Science Monitor.* She is currently a training coordinator for a bank in the Southeast and is serving as a consultant on a picture-book project for the Black Heritage Corp.